Inclusion:
450 Strategies for Success

A practical guide for all educators who teach students with disabilities.

Peggy A. Hammeken

Peytral Publications

Minnetonka, Minnesota 55345

Inclusion: 450 Strategies for Success - A practical guide for all educators who teach students with disabilities.

by Peggy Hammeken

Published by:

Peytral Publications
PO Box 1162
Minnetonka, MN 55345
Tel: 612-949-8707
FAX: 612-906-9777

Cover design: Vanessa Hammeken

Copyright ©1995, 1997 Peytral Publications. All rights reserved.
First, Second, Third, and Fourth Printing 1995
Fifth Printing 1996
Sixth Printing 1997, Revised
Printed and bound in the United States of America

Publisher's Cataloging in Publication
(Prepared by Quality Books, Inc.)

Hammeken, Peggy A., 1955-
    Inclusion: 450 strategies for success: a practical guide for all educators who teach students with disabilities / Peggy A. Hammeken
    p. cm.
    ISBN 0-9644271-7-6

    1. Handicapped children--Education. 2. Mainstreaming in education.
3. Special Education.   I. Title

LC4019.H36 1995   371.9'046
                             QBI94-21160

Library of Congress Catalog Card Number   94-69858

Preface

With the passage of the Education for All Handicapped Children Act of 1975 (PL 94-142) the educational system was faced with the challenge to include all students with disabilities into the classroom setting. Although the law stated that all students were to be educated in the "least restrictive environment," two educational systems emerged. One educational system was called regular, and the second educational system was labeled special. For many years the resource room became the most widely used option for students with disabilities. The students were allowed to be mainstreamed with peers only when deemed appropriate by the special education team or when specific educational criteria had been mastered.

The practice of educating all children with and without disabilities together in heterogeneous classrooms is referred to as inclusive schooling. The concept of inclusion is different from mainstreaming in several ways. Inclusion allows the student to exercise their basic right, the right to be educated with their peers. With inclusion, services are provided to the student within the classroom setting, even if the goals of the student are different from the goals of their peers. With inclusion the student is removed from the classroom setting only after modifications, strategies and support have been provided to the student within the classroom setting. With inclusion, there is no longer a need to integrate the student back into the classroom, because the student has never been removed.

Throughout the United States school districts differ in their acceptance, commitment and implementation of inclusive practices. School districts must begin to define their philosophies. Regular and special education must plan together for the participation and social integration of the student with disabilities.

As the students in the regular education setting become increasingly diverse, curriculum and materials must be adapted, modified and changed to accommodate all learners.

When writing a book the author must develop a philosophy about the subject. It is this author's belief that:

Inclusion can improve the educational system. With inclusion, the modifications and the strategies directed toward students with disabilities are beneficial to other students in the mainstream setting as well. These strategies help to improve and individualize the curriculum for all students within the classroom setting.

Inclusion helps students gain a sensitivity to and an acceptance of all students. When students with special needs are included in the classroom setting, all students will benefit. All students learn to accept one another as contributing members of society regardless of their abilities or disabilities.

Inclusion encourages effective collaboration. No longer is the current educational system fragmented into two separate systems. In an inclusionary setting, all members of the educational team work collaboratively to reach a common goal.

This book is a collaborative effort on the part of many educators, students, parents and administrators. The ideas have been compiled from actual experiences in inclusionary settings. It would be difficult to name individually all the people over the past years who have contributed ideas to this book.

I would like to acknowledge the Eden Prairie School District (Eden Prairie, MN) for providing support and encouragement to staff involved in inclusionary settings. I would like to thank Jan Krmpotich. Without Jan, this book would never have been put on paper. Her support and enthusiasm over the past several years has been immeasurable. I would especially like to thank John Clay, Pam Coffman, Sally Endris, Linda Jiran, Steve Johnson, Jeanne Palmer, Stephanie Rodesch, Peggy Simenson, Kathy Ruemmele, Sue Miller, Janice Tieva and Dr. Lorraine Moore. Their contributions and ideas were the building blocks from which this book was created. I would like to acknowledge Bob Hallett for his administrative support and guidance.

I would like to also acknowledge my family. Vanessa and Melissa provided encouragement and contributed ideas throughout all stages of the book. This book would not have been possible without my husband, Roberto. Countless hours were spent formatting and working on the layout of the book. His enthusiasm and support were always apparent, even during the difficult stages of the book.

This book is dedicated to my mother, Marlene (1934-1992), who taught me at an early age that all people are equal, regardless of their ethnic background, religion or disability.

Table of Contents

Introduction

Inclusion! Does the word bring about feelings of excitement and adventure, or does it lead to feelings of fear, anxiety and apprehension? Conceivably, it may generate a combination of both positive and negative feelings. No matter what the feelings are be assured all teachers have experienced the same range of emotions at one time or another. The strong feelings associated with the word inclusion are not necessarily related to the idea of the integration of students into the classroom. Most educators believe the majority of the students with disabilities do belong in the classroom. The strong feelings directed toward inclusion are usually related to the process of transition and how to manage the transition effectively. The dual educational system that has been in existence for so many years must merge. This is a slow process and it will not happen automatically. It will take time, energy, a willingness to change, and, most of all, an internal belief that inclusion is truly the best for all students.

This book is designed to focus on inclusion of the student with disabilities in the classroom. The first section of the book contains tips about setting up an inclusionary program. The planning and implementation stage is crucial to the success of an inclusionary setting, yet this stage is frequently overlooked. This section will provide you with the assistance you will need to develop an inclusion plan to meet the needs of your school. If you already have an inclusion program, you will find many ideas that will help you improve or expand your existing program.

The second section of the book includes hundreds of ideas and tips for modifying the daily curriculum and strategies that will allow the student to be successful in the classroom. A majority of the modifications listed can be applied to different subject areas and adapted to several areas of the curriculum.

The final section of the book includes an Appendix with reproducible worksheets to assist you with inclusion. These worksheets may be used as they appear in the book or they may be adapted to fit the individual needs of your program.

The ideas presented in this book are numbered for your convenience. When planning, write down the number of the idea you would like to try. This number will allow you to reference the idea quickly. It will save you time and effort while planning for each student. After implementing the ideas, note the ideas that have worked. Do not discard the unsuccessful ideas because they may be appropriate for the next student. Create files and keep the materials for future use. Coordinate a central file of materials at a district level so that teachers may share ideas and modifications between buildings within the district. Look at resources you already have in your district and do not forget to tap into people resources who are available in your community. Good luck with your inclusive program!

Chapter One

Getting Started

Have you ever wanted to include a student into the classroom setting but have been unable to because of scheduling difficulties? Have you encountered times when a student should be included into the classroom but extra support was not available? These concerns are frequently expressed by many educators. Inclusionary settings do not just occur. Proper implementation of an inclusion program will take time, preparation and planning. Due to the growing number of students served in special education, the students must be clustered into classrooms in order for inclusion to be successful. By clustering the students the special education teacher or inclusion assistant will be better able to meet the needs of the student in the mainstream setting.

Ideally, an inclusion program should be developed and set up in the spring for the upcoming school year. If the school year has already started, implement some of the strategies and modifications with a small number of students. If you have an existing inclusion program, you will find this chapter is full of ideas to assist you in improving your existing program.

This chapter will outline a basic plan for the implementation of a successful inclusionary setting. The Appendix also includes several worksheets to assist you with the organization of the program.

Developing a Plan

The inclusion plan should meet the needs of the students, the parents, the staff and incorporate the philosophy of the school district. Every plan will look different due to the unique needs of individual students, the schedule of the school in which you work and the philosophy of the district.

Before you incorporate an inclusion program into your school, it would be helpful to do the following:

1. Visit schools in your area that currently have inclusionary programs. Talk with teachers who have been involved with inclusionary settings. Write down the successful ideas. Learn from the negative experiences of others.

2. Read current research, journal articles and books relating to inclusion. Become familiar with what advocates and critics say about inclusion.

3. List benefits and possible barriers to an inclusion program within your building. Worksheet numbers 2 and 3 in the Appendix will assist you.

4. If you have never worked in an inclusion setting, target one grade level or one specific subject area you feel an inclusion program can be implemented.

5. Formulate an idea you perceive will fit your school and the vision of your school district.

Grouping of Students

In all successful inclusion models, the students are grouped. Target a specific grade level or subject area in your mind. If you are the only teacher who is interested in setting up an inclusion program, target a grade level or subject area with a large number of students. It will be easier to work with a large number of students at one grade level, instead of smaller groups of students in multiple grade levels. If the entire team is moving towards inclusion, divide the case-loads between the special education teachers. Each teacher should work with the fewest number of grade levels and subject areas as possible.

Many inclusion programs fail because students are placed into multiple classrooms. When students are placed in this manner, there is insufficient time to communicate with teachers or to provide sufficient modifications for the various classrooms on a regular basis.

As you read through the next section, think about your target group of students. You will need to experiment with various groups before you will find one that best suits your situation. Not all students will fit into "perfect" groups, but you must find a grouping you feel will be manageable. The following suggestions will offer guidelines for student grouping. Choose the grouping that will best meet the needs of your students.

6.   Review the Individualized Education Plans for all of the students. Analyze each students' strengths. This will assist you with the grouping of students. While reviewing the files, write down area(s) of service, number of minutes and amount of assistant time required by the IEP. You will need to refer to this information while you are developing your plan. Use Worksheets 4 and 5, located in the Appendix to assist you.

7.   When formulating your building plan, group the inclusion students at each grade level into the fewest number of classrooms possible. A recommendation would be to cluster four or five students per classroom. With this grouping, the communication time will increase as will the amount of direct service you will be able to provide to the individual students throughout the school day.

8.   There are several options to consider when grouping students into classrooms. Consider the following options:

   * Academic needs
   * Reading levels
   * Learning styles

* Math placement
* Problem solving skills
* Work habits
* Organizational skills
* Behavioral goals and objectives
* Content or subject area

9. When grouping by reading levels, keep in mind that the students who need minimal modifications may be able to work with an inclusion assistant, if little or no reteaching is required. Use Worksheets 6 and 7 in the Appendix to assist you with groupings.

10. Group students that receive adaptive physical education, speech or language, occupational therapy, physical therapy or other related services. Coordination of these related services will be easier. Merge the language service into an academic block. Occupational therapy services will provide support to the written language block or the handwriting programs. The adaptive physical education teacher may lend support to the regular physical education teacher.

11. Group students that have daily monitoring of organizational skills or participate in a daily check-in or check-out program with the school social worker, counselor or special education teacher.

12. If there are students currently in the due process system who may qualify for special education services, include these students into the groups.

13. If there are new students, make sure their file is reviewed for special education services before the student is placed into a classroom.

Inclusion Assistant Time

Now that you have grouped the students into classrooms, it is time to determine the amount of assistant time necessary for each group. A comment heard frequently when students are not grouped is, "We simply do not have enough assistants to cover all of these students." When students are not grouped, inclusion assistants are assigned to various classrooms for relatively short periods of time. In many cases, when the inclusion assistant arrives the classroom teacher has not yet completed the instruction portion of the lesson. The inclusion assistant is then faced with two choices: either the student is pulled out and misses part of the instruction, or if the inclusion assistant waits for the lesson to finish, the student will not receive the required service that is indicated on the Individual Education Plan.

When the students are grouped and the inclusion assistants are placed strategically within these groups, more direct service will be provided to the students, and support will be increased for the classroom teachers. The inclusion plan needs to be created with the allotment of assistant time that has been determined on the IEP. You must be able to communicate with the assistants and the classroom teachers on a daily basis. Classroom teachers must be able to communicate with the inclusion assistants on a daily basis. The fewer people involved in the program, the more efficient the program becomes. Communication is the key to successful inclusion.

14. Consider assistant time carefully. Strategically place pupil assistants assigned to students, into classrooms where other students will benefit from the service.

15. Students who need daily modifications of the assignments, curriculum support, or reteaching may be grouped with an inclusion assistant. An inclusion assistant cannot provide the direct initial instruction, but the inclusion assistant will be able to reteach skills the classroom teacher has taught, make curriculum modifications and provide support with daily assignments.

16. If there are blocks of open time in the inclusion assistant(s) schedule(s), mark it as "flexible time". Once the program is

implemented, classroom teachers may use this time to provide additional support for the students with special needs.
In this manner, support can be extended to other curriculum
areas.

17. Some school districts will allow the inclusion assistants to
    use flexible scheduling. The inclusion assistant is employed
    for a set number of hours per week. The hours are used as
    needed and may change on a daily basis. This system will
    increase the flexibility of the program.

18. Schedule 10 minutes per day for the inclusion assistant and
    regular education teacher to meet and plan.

19. Write a tentative schedule for the inclusion assistant(s). The
    schedule should include the number of hours that you will
    require for the plan. Refer to the number of minutes on the
    Individualized Education Plan. Worksheet 8 located in the
    Appendix will assist you in the calculation of the assistant
    hours.

Scheduling

Now it is time to structure the day. You will need copies of each of the
classroom teachers' schedules. Read the ideas about scheduling several times
to get an overall feeling on how to structure the school day. Look at sample
Worksheet 9 in the Appendix for ideas. Worksheet 10 is a blank worksheet.
It will give you a basic outline from which to work.

Once classroom teachers volunteer to be part of the program, there will
be changes, but these changes will be worked out between the inclusion team
members.

20. The majority of students will receive service for the reading
    and written language blocks. It is important to stagger these
    time blocks on the schedule so you will be able to provide
    direct service in each of the inclusion classrooms. If two of

the classes have the same reading and language arts block, group the students that work with an inclusion assistant in one of the blocks and schedule yourself in the other academic block.

21. It is important for the special education teacher or the inclusion assistant to be in the classroom during instruction time. This allows the classroom teacher maximum flexibility to monitor and adjust the assignment without having to repeat the directions to the special education teacher or inclusion assistant.

22. Determine the number of students that receive service for math. If your school groups for math, place the students with math goals and objectives into one classroom and plan to team teach with the classroom teacher during this period. If the students are not grouped for math, you will have several options: divide your time between the classrooms, group the students with math IEP's into the same homeroom so you may team teach or use an assistant to assist with the coverage of the various groups.

23. Determine the students' needs for the entire school day. Previously, students' with disabilities have been served mainly in the isolated areas of reading, written language, math and speech/language. These four areas have an impact on the entire school day. Incorporate service into the appropriate academic blocks.

24. Create a flexible time slot in your schedule. It does not need to be a large block of time. The classroom teachers will use this time block to incorporate special projects, lessons, or alternate testing procedures as needed. This time block will also serve as preparation time, observation time or a testing block.

25. Schedule in time each day, before or after school to meet with each teacher. This may be an informal arrangement. Changes in daily lesson plans can be made during this time.

You will be amazed at the number of items that can be discussed during a five minute time block. This is a crucial part of the inclusion program. Lack of communication will cause the program to deteriorate rapidly.

26. Look for ways to incorporate yourself into the classroom. As you become more involved, the students will begin to see you as an integral part of the classroom.

27. If you are able to schedule in a daily preparation time, do so. If not, once the program is implemented, classroom teachers will let you know in advance when they need you. Preparation time will occur during movies, speakers, field trips, art activities or special programs.

Presenting the Inclusion Plan

You have a vision, you have listed the benefits and possible barriers of inclusion, a target group of students has been selected, the assistant time has been carefully calculated in accordance to the IEP's and an outline of a schedule is complete. This is your basic plan. Look it over carefully. You should feel confident in the program and in yourself. You have designed and created a program that you feel will fit the needs of the students and the staff. The time has arrived to present the plan to your principal or supervisor. Submit the outline in a written format. Include all the preliminary data you have gathered. Worksheet 11 located in the Appendix outlines some of the information you may want to include in your presentation. Be prepared to answer any questions that may arise.

Once you have approval, the principal or supervisor will advise you on a procedure to present the program to the staff. This process is critical if the program is to succeed. In this step, you will receive many questions, suggestions and ideas for the program. You will probably need to revise the plan several times during this stage.

28. Write down new questions and ideas from the classroom teachers and administrators.

29. With guidance from your administrator or supervisor, ask several classroom teachers (at the grade level you have targeted) to review the plan. Add their ideas and suggestions.

30. Be open to these new ideas and suggestions. Others will add valuable insights from perspectives that may not have occurred to you. Incorporate these ideas and suggestions. Make the necessary changes. Revise the plan.

31. Present the revised plan to the target grade level. Discuss the benefits of an inclusion program. Discuss the possible barriers you may come across.

32. Present to the staff the proposed schedules that have been developed.

33. Teachers should be made aware that they will need to consult and plan more frequently, especially during the initial stages of the program. Once the program has been implemented and teachers involved learn to collaborate, the amount of time spent in planning and communication will decrease. Communication sessions will decrease in length, but not in frequency.

34. Allow the classroom teachers time to discuss inclusion at their grade level. Be prepared to answer further questions that will arise.

35. Ask for volunteers to work in the inclusion program. Once a teacher volunteers, the teacher will be committed to the success of the program! Commitment is important!

36. A belief that every student deserves to be included in the classroom setting, a positive attitude, enthusiasm, a sense of humor and the willingness to make a change are the key elements of a successful inclusionary program.

In-service and Training

Attitudes play an important role in the success of an inclusion program. Research indicates that in order for a successful inclusion program to take place, all educators must be enthusiastic and ready to implement a change. Research also suggests that attitudes are modifiable and can be altered with proper in-service and training. In-service and training can be provided in many ways. A class or workshop may be taken through local universities or colleges. An introductory class in special education may be beneficial for many teachers. In-service may also take place at the district or building level.

To provide appropriate in-service training, the needs of the building staff must be determined. Use Worksheet 12 to assist in determining the needs of the staff. In-service at the building level should be geared toward the specific needs of the staff and the individual building in which you work.

37. Survey the building staff. The Appendix has a sample survey form to assess the needs and concerns within your building. Design your in-service to meet these needs.

In-service at the building level may be developed around these frequently asked questions.

Overview of Inclusion

* What is inclusion?

* Why is inclusion important?

* What are the federal and state guidelines regarding inclusion?

* What is the district philosophy of inclusion?

* How do we include students in the classroom environment and yet meet all of their needs?

* How do mainstreaming and inclusion differ?

Collaboration Techniques

* What is collaboration?

* What is an effective team?
  How can we work together to form effective teams?

* What are the roles and responsibilities of each person
  in an effective inclusion setting?

* What are various teaching models that can be used in
  a collaborative setting?

* How can we increase the communication in a
  collaborative setting?

Making Modifications and Adapting Curriculum

* What are modifications?

* How do we make modifications to the curriculum?

* How can curriculum be adapted if a large discrepancy exists
  between the classroom materials and the students' current
  levels of performance?

* Who is responsible for making the modifications and
  adapting the curriculum?

Inclusion Assistants in the Classroom

* What are the roles and responsibilities of the inclusion
  assistant in the classroom?

* Who is the primary person responsible to guide the inclusion
  assistant?

* Who is responsible for establishing discipline guidelines for the student in the classroom when an inclusion assistant is present?

* If the student is absent from class, what is the responsibility of the inclusion assistant?

* How will the planning time be incorporated into the inclusion assistant's day?

* How can the inclusion assistant be included in the evaluation of the students?

In-service is an important part of all inclusion programs. Although in-service is highlighted in this chapter, in-service may be provided whenever needed. All in-services do not need to be directed towards the entire staff. Many in-services can be presented in small group sessions as the need arises.

Setting Up an Inclusion Classroom

Once the plan has been initiated you will need to decide how to organize a space within the classroom area. The set up of the classroom depends upon the teaching style of the classroom teacher. There are three types of teaching that usually occur in inclusionary settings. The first is team teaching. In a team teaching environment, two teachers work to plan, develop and teach the lesson. The roles and responsibilities are determined by the teachers. The second type of teaching that frequently occurs in the classroom is supportive teaching. In a supportive teaching environment, the student receives the instruction from the classroom teacher. Modifications and support are provided to the student within the classroom setting by the special education teacher or inclusion assistant. The last form of teaching that may occur is supplemental teaching. In a supplemental teaching environment, the special education teacher or inclusion assistant provides reinforcement and reteaching of the skills as needed. When assignments are not able to be modified or the skill taught is not appropriate, a separate curriculum may also be implemented.

The set up of the classroom environment depends upon the type of teaching system that will be used. The following list will give you some ideas and tips that have worked in inclusionary settings. Use Worksheet 13 located in the Appendix to provide guidelines for setting up the classroom environment.

38. Determine with your colleagues the teaching environment that will best meet the needs of the selected group of students. The teaching strategies will vary throughout the day, depending upon the structure and topic of the lesson.

39. If you anticipate large amounts of supportive or supplemental teaching to take place, establish a teaching area in the classroom. If table space is not available, a quiet area of the classroom with an ample supply of clipboards will work.

40. A table placed outside the classroom is also beneficial. Some students prefer to work in a small group outside the classroom because it may be less distracting. This table may be used by other students or staff if needed throughout the day.

41. A study carrel is useful. This will benefit the student who is easily distracted. Other students will enjoy using it also.

42. When preparing seating charts, seat inclusion students in an area that will allow the special education teacher or the inclusion assistant easy access to the students without disturbing the rest of the class.

43. Designate a specific area in the classroom to leave notes, changes in schedules and other pertinent information.

44. Keep a basket of necessary supplies in each classroom.

45. Purchase a cart and have a classroom on wheels. It's a great way to keep the supplemental materials you need close at hand.

46. A file cabinet placed in a frequently used classroom will help to keep materials and student files close at hand.

47. Since you will be working in various classrooms and your schedule may change daily, you will be difficult to reach by telephone. A telephone beeper or a voice mail service is a practical solution to this problem. Devise a system.

48. A teacher desk may be placed in or near the classrooms. For a successful inclusion program to occur, you will need to be close to the students' classrooms the entire school day.

49. Keep a daily schedule posted in a designated area. This will allow others to find you when necessary.

50. Keep a central file of modified materials and ideas. Store supplemental units and audiocassettes in this file. This will enable the classroom teacher to find materials if you are not available.

51. Develop a professional library of materials to keep in the central location. Include books, reference materials, and community services on the list.

52. Once the program is implemented, make sure you are informed of new students that move into the school during the year. Check their files for special education data. If the student has received special education service in the past or the student may receive special education in the future, group the student into the appropriate classroom.

53. As new students are added during the year, the program will become more complex and schedules will need to be coordinated between more people.

Working as a Team

Educators spend hours each week meeting with parents, colleagues and other adult professionals within the educational system. When the student school day begins, teaching takes on real meaning. The classroom becomes animated with one adult and an active participating audience of students. When the special education teacher or inclusion assistant becomes a part of the group, the dynamics of the entire group may change.

Not all adults are comfortable with another adult in their classroom. Trust will develop. The working dynamics of the inclusion program will change as the comfort level increases. With time one educational team will evolve in place of the two separate educational systems.

54. All teachers have distinct teaching and discipline styles. If there are ideas you would like to share with others, ask the teacher if she/he would mind, before sharing them.

55. Collaboration is important! Special educators and regular educators view situations differently because of their educational backgrounds and experiences. This is important in an inclusion setting! As a special educator you are an advocate for the student with special needs. The regular educator is an advocate for all students in the classroom. If the program is to be successful, educators must learn to collaborate effectively.

56. Make sure that time is scheduled daily to meet with classroom teachers. This time will be used to make changes in lesson plans and/or schedules. Extreme flexibility is very important!

57. If possible, work with the same classroom teachers and inclusion assistants for at least two years. The first year will be a learning experience for everyone. You will be forming a new team, experimenting with new teaching strategies, implementing in-service training for staff and adapting curriculum. You will learn a tremendous amount from trial and error. The second year will be much easier for the team.

You will be part of the team, in-service will be minimal, roles will have been defined, curriculum modifications and adaptations will be in the files and the basic curriculum will be on audiocassettes.

58. In a successful inclusion program, the classroom teachers, parents and students will be your strongest advocates.

Follow Up

Once your inclusion program is established, it is important to obtain follow up information from the teachers, inclusion assistants, parents and students. Follow up questionnaires are a simple method that will allow you to assess the program for each student, parent, inclusion assistant and teacher involved. If the surveys are used frequently, small problems will be discovered before they become problematic. These surveys may also be used as a tool to determine in-service needs. Use Worksheets 14, 15, 16 and 17 to survey the students, parents, inclusion assistants and teachers in the program.

59. Compile the information received from the surveys. If a parent indicates a concern, call to discuss it. Determine whether the concerns expressed by teachers are isolated to a specific classroom or whether it is a program concern and should be addressed as an entire team. Analyze the student surveys. Speak with the students about their concerns. Look at the needs of the inclusion assistants. Determine whether further in-service is needed.

Chapter Two

Modifications for the Student with Special Needs

There is no science to making modifications to the material or the curriculum for students with special needs. Since each student is unique, the students' IEP will provide the framework for the modifications. Look at each student individually in relation to their strengths. When making modifications and adapting the curriculum, the following questions should be addressed:

* What is the goal for this student in this academic area?
* Will this modification assist the student in reaching the final goal?

There are four basic categories for modification of materials:

The activity or content area is reinforced. In this category, the students are provided sufficient support to allow them to experience success with the classroom curriculum. This support will enable the student to complete the classroom assignments and to fulfill the class requirements. Previewing, preteaching or reteaching of assignments may be necessary. Supplemental aids such as study guides, outlines, and audiocassettes of the materials may be provided to the student. The student usually receives their direct instruction from the classroom teacher. The inclusion assistant is able to support these students since direct instruction is provided by the classroom teacher.

The activity or the content area may need to be adapted or modified. In this category, modifications will be made to the actual material or content area of the curriculum. The number of outcomes in a specific content area may be reduced. The student may need extra time to complete the required assignments. Assignments may be shortened. Grading criteria may be modified and assessments will be adapted for the individual student. Instructional groupings may vary. Activities may be presented in large group, small group arrangements or one-to-one if needed. Small group or one-to-one instruction is usually provided by the special education teacher.

A parallel activity may need to be developed. This category of modifications includes the use of supplemental materials and activities where the content may be similar or related to the curriculum. High interest, low vocabulary texts may be used. At this level the functional value of the curriculum will need to be determined and activities created will be similar or related to the curricular content. These activities may be more activity based. At this level, the use of authentic activities and assessments are appropriate. Activities in this group may be planned jointly by the regular education teacher and special education teacher. The plan may be implemented by the special education teacher, the inclusion assistant or the classroom teacher.

The classroom activity is the same, but the final outcome is different. In this category the student may perform the same type of activities as their peer group, but the outcome will be directly related to the student's goals on the Individualized Education Plan. At this level the student may listen to the story from the English textbook with the class, but the student's actual goal may relate to "group socialization". The student may copy a sentence from the blackboard or overhead with the class, but the student's goal may be to develop "fine motor skills". The student may complete subtraction problems using a calculator, but the student's actual goal is to learn to "learn the functions of the calculator" which the student will need to balance a checkbook. The students' goals at this level are functional goals. Functional goals are based on skills the student will need to acquire to live independently as an adult. This independent setting may include a traditional home setting, a supervised apartment or a group home setting.

Curriculum Modifications

The easiest way to illustrate the process of making modifications is to use a hypothetical example. Make a copy of Worksheet 18 in the Appendix. Read this hypothetical example and fill in the worksheet.

John is a 7th grade student with a learning disability. John's ability falls within the average range. John receives special education service in the areas of reading and written language. John's language (both receptive and expressive) is at grade level. John does well in math class and participates in problem solving activities. He is an active participant during group discussions and works well in a cooperative group. John consistently does well on lab experiments in Science class.

Step I: Note John's strengths:
* Average ability
* Receptive and expressive language commensurate with the perceived ability
* Strong aptitude for math
* Participates in class
* Works well in cooperative groups
* Does well with hands-on activities
* Enjoys discussion activities

Since this is a hypothetical situation, the list is short. If this were an actual student, the team would be able to elaborate on these strengths.

Step II: Determine the goals for the subject area.

* John will complete 80% of the social studies assignments.
* John will complete the classroom assessments with at least 70% accuracy.

Step III: Brainstorm possible ideas and strategies that will help John to compensate for his disability. Some ideas may be:

* Provide John with audiocassettes of the social studies text.
* Use cooperative groups during class. Allow John to work with a partner on written assignments.
* Provide John with a study guide for each unit. On the study guide, list the objectives that John will be held accountable for.
* Partner John with a peer during note taking activities. Provide John with a carbon copy of the notes.
* Allow John to take written tests with the special education department or with an assistant. Allow John to demonstrate his knowledge in an alternate form. Oral presentation or final project would be appropriate.

Step IV: Decide the ideas you would definitely like to try. List the person responsible to make the modification. Some modifications, such as creating audiocassettes or typing of study guides may be completed by a volunteer.

This book will save you time, shorten your planning sessions and provide a basis for communication when making modifications for students with disabilities in the classroom. Once Step II has been completed, turn to the Table of Contents in this book. Read through the chapter titles. Determine which chapters are most appropriate for the student. The ideas for modifications have already been compiled for you.

Since the hypothetical student receives support in reading and written language, the following areas were chosen from the Table of Contents:

* Textbook Modifications
* Creating Audiocassettes
* Modifying Daily Curriculum
* Written Language Assignments
* Taking Notes
* Alternate Forms of Assessments

Read through the ideas. Write down the numbers of the specific ideas you would like to try. Decide who will be responsible for creating the modification and who will be responsible to implement the idea. Worksheets 19, 20, and 21 are alternate forms you may use when making modifications.

The strategies, tips and ideas in this book have been used by teachers in inclusive settings. There are hundreds from which to choose! These ideas will contribute to the success of your students in an inclusionary setting!

Chapter Three

Textbook Modifications

"How can the student be included in the classroom, when the student is unable to read the textbook?" Perhaps the question could be rephrased. "How much material will the student be able to learn and/or understand when the information is presented in another manner?" The majority of the students that receive special education services encounter difficulty in the area of reading. Since reading encompasses an enormous portion of the school day, textbook modifications are critical if the student is to experience success throughout the school day.

The modifications listed below are not limited to the reading textbook. Use the following strategies and ideas for science, social studies, English and supplemental textbooks. Whether the student reads the material alone, with support or listens to a tape, always make sure the student is aware that he or she will be held responsible for the follow up activities. Then make sure the student is held accountable.

60. The teacher reads the text aloud to the class using a guided reading procedure.

61. The teacher reads the text aloud to a small group. The students with disabilities are included in the small group. Vary the groups so students become familiar with the small group procedures and become acquainted with their peer group.

62. Divide the students into two groups. The classroom teacher and special education teacher or assistant can read and discuss the information with separate groups. Make sure both teachers have the same outcomes for the lesson. This allows for maximum active participation for all students.

63. Group the students into small groups and allow the students to read aloud. Allow the students to pass or play when it is their turn to read aloud. The student with special needs may not feel comfortable reading aloud at the beginning. As the students comfort level increases, more risks will be taken.

64. Provide the student with outlines of the material to be read. Allow the student to take notes on the outline while the other students are reading.

65. Provide the student with a list of the discussion questions before reading the material. This will assist the student in focusing on important material.

66. Tape record the entire lesson to be read. Allow the student to listen to the tape with a peer. (See the section titled Creating Audiocassettes).

67. Tape record alternate pages of the textbook and allow the student to listen to one page and then read one page either silently or aloud. This will assist the student who is struggling to keep the same pace as his or her peers.

68. Paraphrase the textbook material on tape. Include only the most important material.

69. Discuss the pictures so the student can rely on visual clues while reading.

70. Contact the publisher of the current textbooks used in your school. Many publishers have adapted textbooks that are directly correlated with the grade level textbooks.

Novels and Free Choice Reading

71. Allow students to tape record their favorite books and/or novels. The students may check out these books from the media center or a classroom library and listen to the tape during silent reading time. Allow the student to chose a friend for the activity.

72. While reading aloud to the class, tape record the story. Create a library system in the classroom so students may check out the book along with the tape. Students love to reread the books the teacher has read to them.

73. Allow the inclusion assistant to read aloud to a group of students if there is a non-reader in the classroom. Vary the students in the group.

74. Provide the student with a video tape of the novel or story, before reading, to help build background information for the student.

75. Appoint a student to be *Teacher for the Day*. This student can read aloud a chapter or a story to a small group of students or to an individual student.

76. Provide a collection of novels or stories on audiocassettes from which the student can chose to listen.

77. Choose high interest low vocabulary level books.

Previewing and Preteaching Strategies for Texts

Many students experience success in the classroom if they are allowed to preview the materials before the lesson is actually presented. Previewing and preteaching strategies can be completed with the classroom or special education teacher, the inclusion assistant or at home. These simple techniques produce marvelous results for some students.

78. Allow the student to take home an audiocassette of the material before the material is read in class. This will allow the student to become familiar with the main characters, the story and plot.

79. Allow the student time to preview and discuss the pictures before reading the story. Build background information. Relate new concepts to previously learned concepts.

80. Preview the bold-faced words with the student. Practice reading the words. Define and discuss the vocabulary in context before reading the textbook.

81. Provide a weekly vocabulary list and a list of words in boldface type to the student in advance, so the student is able to read and study the words at home. Use the words in sentences directly related to the context of the text.

82. Generate vocabulary lists for entire textbooks. Include definitions relevant to the text. Include the chapter title and page numbers as a heading. Put this information into a packet. The students may use this packet at home to assist with their homework assignments, unit previews and test reviews.

83. Provide the vocabulary lists from classroom textbooks to the language teachers. This will assist with the coordination of language services into the regular education curriculum.

84. Provide a list of questions to be discussed before reading the text and allow the student to look for the answers. Include page number location clues so the student is able to locate the answers.

85. Highlight important information in the student's textbook. The student or the special education department may purchase the texts for the students. Color code the student textbook. An example would be to use yellow for the vocabulary words, blue for the definitions, and green to highlight topic sentences, facts and important information.

86. Provide an outline of main ideas and vocabulary words for each unit.

87. Teach the student to use the RAP acronym. This will assist the student with paraphrasing of materials. The acronym RAP stands for:

> **R**ead the paragraph
> **A**sk yourself to recall the main idea and several details about what they have read.
> **P**lace the main ideas and important details into your own words.

88. Allow the student to check out a set of textbooks for home use.

Creating Audiocassettes

Audiocassettes are a wonderful tool for students with disabilities. They may be used during the school day or taken home and used for reviewing materials. Once you have the initial tapes, make copies for your grade level or department. Audiocassettes also provide support to the students who have been absent.

89. Use the many sources of volunteers available: parents, peer students, older students, community group members, drama club members, or honor society members to assist when making audiocassettes.

90. When enlisting volunteers to make tapes, examine the reading quality and reading rate of the volunteer before the tapes are made.

91. When preparing audiocassettes, have the speaker read in a clear voice. Eliminate background noise. Texts should be read at 120-175 words per minute.

92. Begin the audiocassette with a statement of the title, the author's name, the chapters, and the sections or the page numbers that are recorded on the tape. Use a consistent labeling system for easy filing.

93. Include study guidelines at the beginning of the audiocassette to orient the student to the main points of the section.

94. List comprehension checkpoints on the tape such as; *"Please stop the tape here and list three uses of water."*

95. Provide special student textbooks that correspond with the tape. Place key symbols in the text that relate to a specific portion of the audiocassette. For example, an asterisk may indicate a portion of the text that has been paraphrased on the audiocassette. A stop sign may indicate that the student should stop and give the definition for a word in bold type. Devise your own system.

96. At strategic points on the audiocassette, ask the student to stop the audiocassette and summarize the information. When the tape restarts, give the student the answer to the question.

97. Provide students with an outline of important material to use as a guide when listening to materials.

98. If including discussion questions on the audiocassette, cue the student to the page numbers where the answers can be found. Answers may also be included on the audiocassette so the student may self check their answers.

99. Paraphrase the entire text, with simplified vocabulary for students who are unable to read. Select the basic concepts you expect the student to master at the beginning of the audiocassette.

Tracking Difficulties

Have you ever worked with a student who is continually losing the place in the textbook? You may feel as though you are always redirecting the student. If this occurs the student is probably experiencing difficulty with visual tracking.

100. Partner the student with a peer and allow the peer to assist the student with visual tracking. Allow students to share a textbook.

101. Give specific instruction as to where the student should begin reading.

102. Give oral clues as to where you are while reading aloud. Redirect the student by pointing out page and paragraph numbers frequently.

103. Seat the student near the teacher so tracking can be easily monitored.

104. Use a bookmark to help the student keep his or her place.

105. Place a horizontal arrow running from the left to the right side of an index card. This will assist the student with directionality.

106. Cut a window into an index card. This will assist the student in focusing because the student is able to see only one line at a time.

107. Provide a picture frame made from construction paper for the student. The student will be able to see several lines of print, yet will be able to block out distracting stimuli.

108. Allow the student to listen to the material and view the pictures while someone else reads the text aloud.

Hearing Impairments

The following suggestions will provide additional support for the student with a hearing impairment.

109. Seat the student near the teacher.

110. Always use visual signals to secure the student's attention when reading aloud.

111. Speak and read clearly in a normal tone and at a moderate pace.

112. Rephrase content areas or questions to make the lesson more easily understood.

113. Provide the student with an outline and vocabulary lists before introducing new material. Encourage the student to preview the information at home before the lesson is presented.

114. Present vocabulary words in sentences. Many words may look similar to lip readers.

115. Repeat and summarize information when presented orally.

116. If the student reads lips, provide the student with a swivel chair, so student will be able to see the teacher and the sign language interpreter at all times.

Vision Impairments

If the student with visual impairments appears to be inattentive or looking around in the classroom instead of at you, the student may be relying on the auditory channel to gain information. Students with visual impairments often experience visual fatigue during classroom assignments. Many materials are available specifically for visually impaired students.

117. Order specialized materials, such as enlarged textbooks, magnifiers, closed circuit television and computer software with enlarged fonts and pictures.

118. Provide audiocassettes for the student's textbooks. Create audiocassettes on cassette players with variable recording speeds. This will allow the student to increase the speed as his or her auditory skills become more refined.

119. Allow the student extra time to complete assignments. Be aware of visual fatigue during activities requiring continuous use of visual skills. Some signs of visual fatigue may include red eyes, rubbing of the eyes, laying the head on the desk and squinting.

120. Minimize fatigue by modifying the number and length of activities that require visual concentration.

121. Questions and comments should be directed to the visually impaired student by addressing the student by name.

122. Tape record the assignments so the students may listen to them as often as needed.

123. When using Braille or new supplemental devices in the classroom, provide in-service for the entire class. Teach the students how to write their names or label various objects in the classroom with Braille. The students will be excited by the newly acquired knowledge. It will become a learning experience for all students.

124. Touch is important for visually impaired students. Provide hands-on experiences whenever possible.

Chapter Four

Modification of Daily Assignments

Whenever a daily assignment is given, the purpose of the assignment should be determined. Most assignments are used to verify the students understanding of the concept presented. Although it is customary to ask the student to respond in a written format, this may not always be possible for students with disabilities. Some students feel overwhelmed, which, in turn, may result in frustration and acting out behaviors. Always determine the outcome of the assignment and then modify the assignment according to the student's needs.

An important question that arises when discussing inclusion is "When will the student receive the remedial support needed if the student is included in the classroom the entire day?" While the students are completing daily assignments in the classroom, it is an optimum time for the student to receive direct instruction from the special education teacher or reteaching with the inclusion assistant. Many daily seat work activities are designed to reinforce previously taught skills or to check for understanding of a specific skill. Determine the appropriateness of the activity. Ask, "Is this beneficial to the student?" and "Is it important for the student to complete the entire assignment?" If not, use the time to provide the student with a supplemental series or use the time to reinforce previously taught skills. If there are other students within the classroom setting who would benefit from reteaching or reinforcement, include these students in the group. Ideas for modifications of daily assignments may also be found under the specific subject areas.

125. Divide the assignment in half. Allow the student to complete the even or the odd problems.

126. Break the assignment into segments and allow the student to complete the assignment over a period of several days.

127. Use a cover sheet with long assignments. The assignment will not seem so overwhelming to the student.

128. Work in cooperative groups or with partners so the student is able to have the questions read aloud to him.

129. Allow the student to respond verbally to the questions into a tape recorder.

130. Provide a photocopy of the material to the student. Allow the student to highlight, underline or fill in the blank on the photocopy instead of copying the entire page of sentences, math problems or the paragraph.

131. Provide an assignment sheet to help the student organize and prioritize daily assignments. Include due dates.

132. Rewrite the materials at an appropriate reading level or provide a parallel activity for the same skill.

133. Allow a partner to write the student's response.

134. Allow the student to respond orally. This works well for the student that is continually behind with class work. The student may respond orally to several of the daily assignments. The student should be held accountable for other written assignments.

135. Provide extra drill and practice sessions for the student. Work towards mastery of the skill. Monitor and adjust the final outcome if necessary.

136. Provide extra time for completion of assignments.

137. Allow the student to illustrate his/her answer instead of responding in a written format.

138. Provide supplementary materials that coincide with the text at an easier readability level. Many teachers' guides include the blackline masters for various levels.

139. Provide parallel activities at an appropriate level. An example would be: If the objective is to locate nouns, use the student's reading text. Allow the student to write the nouns from the story. If the student is unable to read, have the student locate objects in the classroom that are nouns.

140. Provide written contracts for curriculum units. This allows for simple modifications to the length by highlighting the assignment the student with must complete.

141. Provide the student with a package of stick-on notes. The student can write down each incomplete assignment on a separate note. When the assignment is completed, the student may throw the note away. If the assignment is not completed during the school day, the student can place the note in the assignment book at the end of the class.

142. Allow the student to use a computer, word processor or calculator to complete required work.

Chapter Five

Written Language Modifications

Written language incorporates a wide range of skills. Students may encounter difficulty with written language for many different reasons. Some students may encounter difficulty because they are unable to transfer their ideas into a written format. Other students will encounter difficulty with the grammar, syntax, or the mechanics of writing. Still others may experience difficulty due to language limitations or the ability to process language.

<u>Generating Ideas</u>

"I have a student who simply refuses to write," or "I have a student who sits and just stares at the paper. The student refuses even to attempt to write." These concerns are heard frequently among educators. There may be times when a student is so frustrated with writing, and language processing is so difficult, they simply refuse to write. If this happens, allow the student to choose a topic during the journal or the writing session.

143. The student with special needs should be encouraged to write on a daily basis. Journaling is a form of writing that can be completed on a daily basis. A free response, question and answer format or a written response to a special event will encourage the student to write.

144. Give the student specific instructions for the assignment. Gradually decrease the structure as the student becomes more confident in his or her ability to write.

145. If a student has difficulty generating specific ideas, create a student/teacher journal. The teacher can direct specific questions to the student and the student can respond in writing.

146. Allow the student to choose one familiar idea. Generate a word bank and allow the student to write on the same topic for several days.

147. Once the student has generated an idea, assist the student in creating an outline of the story or topic.

148. Keep a selection of pictures available and give the student a picture to help generate ideas.

149. If the student has difficulty generating ideas, request the student to write a minimum number of sentences per day. (You may have to start at one!) Build on the topic each day. The next week increase the goal. Make sure the student is held responsible to meet the individual goal.

150. Have the student bring a picture from home and write about the picture.

151. If the student is unable to generate a sentence, have the student write descriptive words or illustrate the idea. The words may be combined into simple sentences at a later time.

152. Use sequence cards and have the student write a sentence about each step.

153. Use sequence cards and have the student write a sentence about the final step.

154. Allow the assistant to write the student's ideas and the student may copy the idea or story from the model.

The Writing Process

155. Avoid excessive corrections in the mechanical aspects of writing so the student does not become discouraged with the writing process. Give more attention to the development of the ideas than to the mechanics of writing.

156. Teach the student to use mapping skills when writing. The map should include the key ideas and words for the topic. Mapping will also help the student visualize the relationship between the parts of the story. To illustrate mapping, the topic of dogs will be used. In the center of the paper write the word dog. Now divide the paper into four sections. Each section will have words that pertain to some aspect of the dog. Topics for each of the four sections might include: feeding, exercising, grooming and training dogs as pets. When the mapping exercise is complete, the story will be organized for the student. The student has the main topic, four paragraphs and a selection of key words for each paragraph.

157. Before writing a story have the student answer the following questions:

 * Who is the main character?
 * Who else is in the story?
 * What does the main character want to do in the story?
 * What happens when the main character does this?
 * How does the story end?

These simple questions should assist the student with the organization of their thoughts and a basic outline for the story.

158. Teach the student the importance of a beginning, middle and end in each paragraph. Incorporate transition words such as *first, next, then, last* or *finally* when writing paragraphs. It will assist the student with sequencing their thoughts.

159. Teach the student to proofread all assignments. Give the student a checklist form for proofreading. It should include capitalization, punctuation, misspelled words, margins, paragraph indentation and sentence sense. The student should read the entire paper and edit the paper for capital letters. When completed, the student may check it off the form. The second time, the student should read the paper and edit the paper for punctuation. Continue in this manner until the entire paper is proofread.

160. The SPACE strategy may be used as an error monitoring strategy when writing. The acronym SPACE stands for the following:
    * **S**PELLING
    * **P**UNCTUATION
    * **A**PPEARANCE
    * **C**APITALIZATION
    * **E**RROR ANALYSIS

161. Teach the student to self check each area in the SPACE acronym before turning in the assignments.

162. Have the student record or read the story aloud after it has been written. Many students will be able to hear inaccurate sentence construction. Allow the student ample time to make the corrections.

163. Since written language is a form of communication, allow the students to share their stories and reports often. It is important for students to hear good models. Do not require the students to read in front of the class if they do not desire to do so.

164. Allow the student to use a computer or a word processor.

165. Look at the quality of the assignment instead of the quantity produced. When working on topic sentences, details and a closing sentence, allow the student to produce one quality paragraph instead of a series of paragraphs.

166. When working on class reports, allow the student to use a fill in the blank standard form. An example for the topic *Birds* might be:

   My bird is a _____. *He lives in the* _____ *part of the United States. He is* _____ *in color.*

   The student can add as many details as necessary.

167. When writing research papers assist the student with the formulation of the topic sentence. Encourage the student to look for details. Modify the number of sources in the bibliography.

168. Allow the student to present the final project to the class in another format. A videotape, demonstration, display or oral presentation may capitalize on the student's strengths.

Prewriting Stage

With some students there may be a large discrepancy between the student's ability to write and the writing ability of the class. Some students may be in a prewriting stage. If the student is in a prewriting stage, parallel or supplemental activities can be provided according to the student's Individualized Education Plan. The ideas and strategies listed in the Fine Motor section will provide additional support for these students.

169. Allow the student to dictate the story. Write the story for the student. The student can practice reading the story and writing or tracing the letters.

170. Allow the student to dictate their response to a peer. The student can practice reading the story using a language experience approach.

171. Purchase paper with raised lines so the student is able to practice letter and word formation.

172. Write the question and the student's response in pencil. Allow them to trace with a felt tip pen and then illustrate.

173. Have the student copy material from the board or overhead onto paper. The student's final outcome may be different than the outcome of the peer group. In this situation the outcome may be a handwriting goal.

174. Allow the student to illustrate their response instead of writing.

175. Allow the student trace templates to develop fine motor control.

176. Give the student tracing paper and have the student trace large objects from a coloring book.

177. Have the student reproduce simple shapes from a model. Begin with bold line shapes and move into connecting dots and lines.

178. Use the time to practice letter formation. Use clay, sand trays and tracers.

179. Allow the student to work on dot-to-dot pictures. Use both A,B,C and 1,2,3 pictures.

180. Use the time for other fine motor development activities such as stringing beads, pegboard designs, sewing cards, weaving, cutting or clay.

Spelling Difficulties

181. At first glance, due to numerous spelling errors, written language assignments may appear to lack creativity or solid ideas. Allow the student to spell phonetically. Have the student read his/her response to you if necessary. Revise the paper with the student. Give encouragement to all attempts.

182. Choose one or more words the student uses frequently during journal writing. Develop a spelling dictionary of frequently misspelled words for the student.

183. Allow the student to tape record his/her response and then transcribe it later. Teach and encourage the student to use a dictionary and a thesaurus.

Fine Motor Difficulty

Some students have wonderful ideas and are very creative. A delay in fine motor skills may cause difficulty and frustration for the student when transferring the ideas to paper. Instead of allowing the creativity to flow, the student may write in short, choppy sentences to compensate for the difficulty in fine motor control. Interestingly, when the obstacle of writing is removed, these students may become some of your most creative students.

184. Check the student's pencil grip. Place adhesive tape or a pencil grip on the pencil.

185. Provide various sizes of wide ruled paper. Begin with the large ruled size and slowly decrease the size of the paper until the student is using grade level paper. If the correct size of paper is unavailable commercially, create the appropriate size using lined paper and a felt tipped pen. Photocopy it.

186. Write the student's answer or story in pencil and allow the student to trace it with a marking pen.

187. Provide a close-up model for the student to copy, instead of the board or overhead.

188. Provide an alphabet card or alphabet strip so the student is able to see the correct formation of the letters. Allow the student to use manuscript or cursive, depending on the student's preference.

189. If appropriate, write the assignment for the student. The parents should also be made aware of your expectations regarding homework assignments. Indicate under which circumstances the homework assignment may be written for the student.

190. Modify the length of the assignment. If the assignment is long, break it into sections and allow the student to complete one portion at a time over a period of several days if necessary.

191. Look at the quality of the assignment produced instead of the quantity produced.

192. Provide the student with a word processor or a lap top computer or to use with long assignments.

Chapter Six

Spelling

Spelling words should be compatible with the reading level of the student. Modifications for spelling may be as simple as modifying the length of the list or they may be complex, such as creating an appropriate spelling program. For the student who is not yet ready for a formal spelling program, students can use the time to develop fine motor activities, letter formation, and sound/symbol relationships. The student will make a gradual transition into a spelling program. If the student is able to phonetically blend two sounds, a formal spelling program can be implemented.

Grade Level Spelling Lists

Many students with disabilities can succeed in the regular spelling curriculum with minimal modifications.

193. Modify the classroom spelling list by adjusting the number of items on the list.

194. Allow the student to set an individual spelling goal.

195. Increase the number of words when the student reaches mastery level on three consecutive tests. (Check the Individualized Educational Plan)

196. Group the spelling words into word families so the student is able to focus on the pattern.

197. If the student is unable to read a large number of the words on the list, delete some of the unfamiliar words. Insert commonly used sight words or words that follow the current word patterns.

Creating Spelling Lists

198. When creating supplemental spelling lists, the list should be consistent with the student's reading level. Incorporate words from the student's basal reader when creating a supplemental spelling program.

199. Choose spelling words that are relevant to the curriculum and consistent with the student's vocabulary.

200. Select a word bank from the student's basal reader. Group the words according to word families or if using a sight word approach, by the number of letters in the word.

201. Create leveled spelling lists on the computer, using the same format as the spelling text. The student is able to use the same practice pages as their peers even though their list may contain different words.

202. Use the previous year's spelling list and adapt it to the format of the current grade level spelling list.

Parallel Spelling Activities

Not all students are ready for a formalized spelling program. Some students may need parallel activities. These activities may be completed alone, with a peer or with the special education assistant.

203. Create a spelling list of consonant sounds that coincide with the initial letters sounds of the class spelling list. The student is able to work on sound association and letter formation.

204. Have the student write the initial consonant sound as peers write the entire word.

205. Begin with basic sight words and simple phonetic words such as *a, at, am* and *an* as soon as the student knows several letters and sounds.

206. Begin spelling with the student's proper name along with the names of family members, friends, peers or pets. Develop the spelling list from the sentence. Practice the sentence until mastery has been reached. This lesson may be incorporated into spelling, handwriting or used as a written language activity. An example would be:

<u>List</u>
my
Meg
is
My name is Meg.
Meg is my name.

207. Provide the student with practice pages of the words and sentences. The student may trace the words or sentences with multiple colors of crayons, felt tipped pens or fine tip markers.

208. Provide practice sheets the student can trace. Use peers to drill and monitor the student's progress.

Drill and Practice

Drill and practice activities take place daily in the classroom. Vary the assignments. Make sure that the student is held accountable for meeting the daily goals.

209. Group the word lists into word families.

210. Group the words that contain the same prefixes and suffixes to teach patterns. Teach the spelling and meaning of the suffixes and prefixes in isolation.

211. Provide highlighters so students can highlight base words, suffixes or prefixes to aid in visual discrimination.

212. Teach only one spelling rule at a time.

213. Provide the student with a close up model to from which to work. Many students experience difficulty when copying unknown words from a distant model.

214. Combine spelling and handwriting goals to allow time for extra drill and practice.

215. Allow a minimum of ten minutes structured practice time daily. Students who experience difficulty with organizational skills will need this time to find and organize their materials.

216. Do not require all students to practice all words daily. It may be too overwhelming. Allow the student to practice two or three words per day if the student is frustrated by a long list.

217. Provide drill and practice exercises such as spelling bingo, hangman, word finds and spelling baseball.

218. Vary the daily drill and practice exercises. Along with paper and pencil tasks, allow the student to practice on the chalkboard, in small groups, or do it orally on tape.

219. For younger students practice with shaving cream, sand trays, fingerpaints or write the words in pudding.

220. Provide the student with an audiocassette of the word list. The student can practice alone during extra class time or take the tape home. This audiocassette may also be used if a student needs to retest or was absent during the test. Tape record the words while pretesting to save time.

221. Provide word strips for the student to trace with crayon or marker. This will provide drill and practice for correct letter formation. Trace each word with three or four colors.

222. Encourage the student to verbalize the initial sounds while writing the words.

223. Allow the student to practice on a typewriter, computer or word processor.

224. Assist students to use mnemonic devices and configuration clues to recall correct spelling.

225. Allow students to choose the study method that works best for them.

Study Methods for Spelling

For students with disabilities the most effective method is a method which will capitalize on the students' strengths. Three guidelines for studying spelling are listed here.

Visual Learners

226. This method focuses on the student's visual strength. This method is appropriate for students with a hearing impairment or students who rely on visual patterning.

   * The student should view the word while the teacher reads the word aloud to the student or the entire class.
   * The student studies the word by reading it, spelling it, and reading it again.
   * The student attempts to spell the word orally two times with out the model.
   * Finally, the student attempts to write the word without the model.

Auditory Learners

227. If the student relies heavily on auditory skills to learn new words, the following steps may be implemented into the spelling program. This method should be used for students with a visual impairment.

   * The student should observe the teacher reading, spelling and writing the word.
   * The student should read the word and attempt to repeat the letters verbally after the teacher.

* Once again the student should listen to the teacher spell the word and the student should repeat it after the teacher.
* The student spells the word without assistance.

Multisensory Approach

228. A cover and write method is appropriate for the student who needs a multisensory approach.

* The student looks at the word and pronounces it.
* The student spells the word aloud.
* The student covers the word and writes it down.
* The student compares their work to the model.
* If the student has written the word correctly, the student will practice the word three times.
* A final check is made. If all the words are correct, the student is ready to go on to the next word.

229. Allow the student to experiment with various programs. The student will be able to choose a study method that will best meet their individual needs.

230. Allow the student to practice with a peer, teacher or assistant to ensure the student is practicing the words correctly. Spot check frequently if the student is practicing alone.

Spelling Tests

Many students with disabilities not only need to learn the spelling of the word, but in many situations, the student may need to learn to read the word, also.

231. Test the student orally instead of in writing. Give the student an index card or paper with the score to turn in to the classroom teacher.

232. Write the response for the student. This will provide assistance to the student with fine motor difficulty.

233. Cue the student as to the number of letters in each word when working with silent letters. This will help the phonetic speller to include the silent letters.

234. Test students over several words daily instead of one final test.

235. Allow the student to take the test with the special education teacher or the inclusion assistant if appropriate.

236. With the lower functioning student allow the student to select the correct spelling flashcard that corresponds with the word that has been read.

237. If the student needs long periods of time to process information, give the student the test on an audiocassette. The student will be able to stop the tape and think about the word for as long as needed.

238. If the student reverses letters frequently, ask the student to spell the word orally. Give the student credit for each correct response.

Grading

239. Record pretest and posttest scores. Grade on effort and improvement in place of percentage.

240. Allow students to self monitor their spelling progress by charting pretest and posttest scores. Many students are motivated by self-monitoring techniques.

241. Have the student set a weekly goal. Reward the student if his/her individual goal is met even if the student does not obtain the required class percentage.

242. Be sure to adhere to changes in grading or criteria noted on the Individualized Education Plan.

Chapter Seven

Mathematics

The difficulties a student experiences in math may be directly related to the areas of auditory and visual processing, sequencing of steps or rote memory. The majority of math problems require multiple, sequential steps in order to produce the correct answer. Confusion often results when there are numerous steps involved to complete one math problem. With basic math, students with disabilities may require the use of concrete materials such as manipulatives. When using manipulatives the student must first complete the operation using the concrete materials. Once the student obtains an answer, the student must retain the answer in the short term memory in order to transfer the answer to paper. Since many students with disabilities may also have difficulty with short term memory, this is no easy task.

When providing service to the student with disabilities in the math setting, you will also want to refer to the chapters entitled Modifications of Daily Assignments and Testing Procedures. Both of these chapters have many practical ideas to support the student in the area of mathematics.

General Teaching Strategies

243. Many students with disabilities experience difficulty with abstract concepts. Introduce math concepts in "real life" situations. This relationship will help students understand the relevance of the lesson. Several examples that would

provide meaning for the student may include: introduce percentages and graphing by using the statistics of the school sports teams, addition, subtraction and decimals may related to balancing a checkbook, measurement and fractions may be introduced with cooking, time concepts may be related to class schedules or television programs. These examples of practical math will provide relevance and meaning to the subject of mathematics. Brainstorm and list the ideas at the beginning of the year. Each time a new concept is taught, refer to the original list.

244. When teaching a mathematical concept, do not worry about perfect calculations. The student must first understand the process.

245. Teach key math terms separately. Provide the students with a dictionary of math terms. Include drawings and examples to illustrate the various steps of the problems.

246. When teaching abstract concepts, use drawings, diagrams and visual demonstrations to help the student establish a visual and concrete relationship.

247. Use colored chalk or colored pens when demonstrating assignments. This will direct the student's attention to the important points. An example would be to color code the groups of ones, tens, or hundreds. Another example would be to color code the number that has been regrouped to draw attention to the number.

248. Highlight similar math operations on each page to help the student focus on the operation.

249. Cluster math problems into groups. If the assignment includes several types of math calculations on one page, the student should complete all the same operation before preceding on to the next. For example, the student should complete all the multiplication problems before moving on to division problems.

250. Teach the student the math fact families. This will help to establish the relationship between numbers.

251. If applicable, model the math problem using manipulatives. When modeling, explain each step verbally to the student. Instruct the student to verbalize each step while practicing the procedure. Listen to the student verbalize the problem. You will be able to understand the student's thinking process and analyze which step in the process is giving the student difficulty.

252. When teaching strategies for numberlines, draw a number-line on the floor for the students may walk on. This will also assist the student with directionality.

253. If a student is unable to grasp the numberline concept, use counters, cubes, popsicle sticks or buttons.

254. When teaching the concept of money, it is best to use real money instead of paper or cardboard money.

255. If using timed tests, reduce the number of problems or increase the time limit. Provide ample workspace on the worksheet.

256. In place of timed tests, use computer programs. In many commercial math programs the time and the number of problems may be preset.

257. Allow the student to graph the information from timed tests. Look for improvement. Most timed tests only cause frustration for students with mild disabilities.

258. Frequently review and reinforce previously taught skills. Use daily quizzes.

259. Many students with disabilities need immediate feedback on their assignments. Create several different work stations. Include student activities with self correction sheets.

260. When teaching word problems, simplify the vocabulary. Leave out irrelevant information. Teach the key words that are associated with word problems. When teaching word problems it is helpful to do the following:

Ask the student to read the problem to determine the question.
Reread the word problem. Look for key words in the problem. Some of the key words are: altogether, together, in all, are left, spent or remain.
Draw a diagram of the word problem.
Write out the problem. Estimate the answer before solving it. If the answer seems reasonable, solve the problem.

261. Develop task analysis sheets for the basic areas of mathematics. Use these checklists to determine the specific area of difficulty. Look for patterns of errors in daily assignments. Have the student verbalize the process to you. Some students will experience difficulties because they miss one step in the process or they are performing one step incorrectly. Patterns of errors usually emerge in the following areas: inadequate knowledge of facts, incorrect operations, or the use of ineffective strategies.

Parallel Math Activities

Some students will not be able to complete the same curriculum as the rest of the class. For these students it is important to be aware of the goals and objectives on the Individualized Educational Plan. Supplementary skills can be provided for the student in the classroom that correspond with the class activity. Listed below are just a few ideas of activities that could be completed with a peer or an assistant.

262. Decide whether the skill is a "functional" life skill. Make sure the skills taught are skills that will support the student in independent living.

263. Provide supplemental skills in the same content area as the rest of the class. For example, if the class is learning addition with regrouping, the student may work on basic addition facts with an assistant. It is possible the student can still be involved in the discussion, demonstration and use the manipulatives, if the classroom teacher varies the questions and directs specific questions toward the student

264. Correlate the objectives from the Individualized Education Plan with the instruction. If the student is working on number recognition, use the classroom daily assignment or the textbook. If the objective is for the student will be able to write numbers, the student could write the numbers from the textbook.

265. Order a supplemental text for the student's direct instruction. Direct instruction can be provided for the student while the rest of the class is receiving instruction. During seat work time, the student will be able to complete the assignment in the supplementary text.

266. Use dot-to-dot activities for number sequencing and number recognition.

267. Work on number formation with the use of tracers and/or templates.

268. Give the student number cards. Work on the chronological sequencing of numbers. Use the same cards for one-to-one correspondence, ordering from least to greatest or number recognition.

269. Make cards for mathematical symbols. Have the student put them together into correct mathematical equations. The student may copy the equation onto paper.

270. Collect shells, beads, seeds, various shaped pasta and buttons. Put them into boxes or bags. Use these collections to sort and classify objects. The materials may also be used to assist with one-to-one correspondence.

271. Use egg cartons to sort various materials and establish the concept of *group*. Use this concept of group to introduce addition and subtraction.

272. Teach the student to use a calculator. Allow the student to do some of the problems in the text with a calculator.

273. Have the student collate the papers in chronological order.

274. Coordinate the students assessments, seat work time and rewards with the mainstream math class.

275. Create games the student may play with other students in the classroom. Vary the peer group.

Modifying Math Assignments

276. Place arrows on the student's worksheet to assist with directionality. Many students will try to perform math calculations from left to right instead of right to left.

277. Draw dotted lines between the columns of math problems so the student is able to record the information in the correct column.

278. Box in the ones column so the student knows where to begin the math calculation.

279. Turn lined paper vertically so the student has ready made columns. Use graph paper for instant organization of math problems.

280. Purchase consumable texts from the publisher if available. Students with fine motor difficulty will not have to copy problems and will be able to spend more time with the actual calculations.

281. If consumable texts are unavailable, enlarge the text so the student may write on the photocopied page.

282. When working with problem solving activities, emphasize the problem solving steps, not the final answer. Many students do not participate for fear their final computation is incorrect.

283. Number the steps in word problems. Highlight the important words.

284. Allow the student to use charts, graphs and tables when the process of addition, subtraction, multiplication and division is understood.

285. When using addition, subtraction or multiplication charts, provide the student with a cutout "L". This will assist the student to find the intersection box of columns and rows.

286. Provide the student with ample time to memorize the basic facts before using the calculator.

Student Aids

287. When teaching multiple step math calculations, write down the steps of the process for students to use as a guide. Provide a visual model next to the written steps so the student can see the correlation between the model and the written problem. Division is an example of a process that requires multiple steps.

288. Create a small booklet for the student to keep as a math reference book. The booklet should include the basic math concepts covered in the class. The student can then refer to the guide if he/she is confused about a mathematical operation. Include the math terminology and a visual diagram for each step.

289. Attach a numberline to the student's desk or in the math book. This will assist the student with addition, subtraction and the correct formation of the numbers. This will also assist students who experience difficulties with number reversals.

290. Teach the student to use the face clock in the classroom as a number line for facts to 12. This will support the student who is adverse to having a numberline placed on the desk.

291. Create a chart with two numberlines. Label one for addition with an arrow to the right and label the other chart for subtraction with an arrow running to the left. This will help the student internalize the concept.

292. Allow the student to use rubber number stamps if number formation is extremely difficult.

293. Allow the student to use a calculator for all math calculations once the process and the concept are mastered.

294. Apply strategic points to the numbers. Teach the students to count the points to arrive at the correct answer.

295. Use stick-on notes to help the student keep his/her place in the text.

Chapter Eight

Organizational Skills

"I can't find my homework. I know I turned it in! I know I did it!" Do these phrases sound familiar?

Students with disabilities are often able to complete assignments when adapted to their specific needs, but they may continually lose or misplace the completed work. Others students experience difficulty with organization of time and physical space. Still others may be unorganized because they are unable to follow oral and written directions. (See the section on directions.) This section will focus on organization of the physical environment of the student.

<u>Classroom Organization</u>

296. Provide the student with a simplified map of the school. Number and highlight the classrooms and the most direct route for the student.

297. Write a daily schedule on the board and follow it as closely as possible. Some students need to anticipate what will occur next in the school day.

298. Organize the classroom so there is one location to hand in daily assignments.

299. Develop a classroom routine and follow it. If possible, take breaks at approximately the same time each day. Allow the student several extra minutes to organize materials.

300. Color code folders for each subject. If possible coordinate folders with the colors of the textbook.

301. Keep all of the student supplies in a central area. Clearly state what the student may use during the day.

302. Create seating arrangements that allow the student to see the board easily without turning their body.

Student Organization

303. Use color coded folders for academic areas. Keep a pencil, pen, paper and other necessary items in each folder.

304. If folders are confusing for the student, use a three ring notebook. Keep all folders and paper in one notebook. The student should never remove any paper unless it is time to turn it in to the classroom teacher. If the papers are loose, use a three ring hole punch. Once the papers are punched they can be inserted into the notebooks. This is great for the student who has extreme difficulty with organization.

305. Have the student clean and organize his/her desk or locker at least once a week. Organize papers into three piles: file into folders, take home or toss.

306. Make sure the student places a heading on all papers. This will assist the student in storing papers in the appropriate folder.

307. Develop a color code chart and post it, or have the student keep a crayon that matches the corresponding folder and

color code the corner of each assignment. With written assignments, it is easy to confuse a social studies rough draft report with an English rough draft report.

308. Incorporate classroom discussion about organization into the curriculum. Allow the students to share their ideas and organizational strategies. List the ideas. Many students need to be taught organizational skills.

309. Use a homework book or an assignment sheet. Teach the student how to prioritize assignments. Some students need a weekly or monthly calendar to understand the concept of time.

310. List assignments and the approximate length of time that will be needed to complete the assignment. This will assist the student with prioritizing the classwork.

311. Supply the student with a pad of "Things to Do Today". Teach the student how to write reminders to him/herself.

312. Use a peer to help monitor assignments. The peer can assist the student in placing assignments in correct folders or turning in assignments.

313. For students that have difficulty remembering to do homework, allow the student to call home and leave a message on a recorder, if available. Make sure the student notes the subject and page numbers if applicable.

314. Allow the student to check out an extra set of textbooks for home use.

315. Give the student a packet of stick-on notes. The student can write down each assignment as given. The note can be placed on the student's desk. The student may throw the note away when the assignment is complete or stick it into the homework notebook.

316. Create a simple daily checklist. The student can tape onto the top of his/her desk or into a notebook. Write down the assignments with the due dates. The student can cross off the assignment when completed.

317. When an assignment has been completed, encourage the student to turn it in immediately. It can be very frustrating for the student to redo an assignment because it is lost.

318. Plastic bags work well for extra pencils, crayons, markers and supplies. The student can keep several individual bags of supplies.

319. Give extra time to students with organizational difficulties to find their materials before presenting new materials. Many students will miss directions because they are still looking for supplies.

320. If assisting students with check-in and check-out on a daily basis, go into the student's classroom. The student will not miss valuable class time or important directions. You may also use the time to double check any assignments listed on the board.

321. Teach the student to use self-talk methods. The student should verbalize the steps after the teacher has given a multi-step direction.

322. Enlist parent cooperation in setting up a specific time each day for homework. If the student does not have home-work, the student may spend the time reading, or cleaning and organizing their folders or backpack.

323. Hanging folders, numbered manilla folders, file folders or mailboxes may be set up in the classroom. Papers may be placed immediately into the folder for storing or taking home.

Chapter Nine

Directions

Each day students must process hundreds of directions. Many students with disabilities experience difficulty in school because they are not able to process directions. Inattention, difficulty with auditory processing, memory deficits, poor listening skills, limited receptive language or the inability to sequence information are only a few of the reasons. No matter what the root of the problem is, it can be a very frustrating experience for the student.

Oral Directions

324. Make sure you have the student's attention before giving directions. Pause and wait if you do not. Eye contact is important.

325. Change the format of oral directions. Provide directions in written format so the student is able to refer back to it.

326. Do not give irrelevant information during an oral direction. Keep directions concise and simple.

327. Simplify the vocabulary.

328. Accompany verbal explanations with a visual demonstrations whenever possible.

329. Break the direction into one and two step components. If the directions are complex, allow the student to complete the first several steps before giving more directions.

330. Appoint a peer tutor to coach the student through multiple step directions.

331. Have the student repeat the direction back to you or a peer to check for understanding.

332. Use a combination of visual and auditory directions for the student. Use the blackboard, the overhead or a flip chart.

333. Include rebus pictures with written directions for students who are unable to read the directions.

334. Photograph the steps of experiments, demonstrations and multiple step activities. Place photographs in chronological order in a file folder. The student may use this folder when a visual aid is needed. File directions with the unit for future use.

335. Record daily assignments on tape. The student may listen to the directions as many times as needed. Include the due dates. Encourage the student to write down incomplete assignments into a homework notebook.

336. If the student has a hearing impairment, appoint a peer to cue the student when oral directions are given. Be sure the student is cued into messages given on the intercom. Always check for understanding.

Written Directions

337. Provide directions in sequential order. If there are multiple steps, number the steps.

338. Allow student time to copy the assignment. If the student is unable to copy from a distance, allow him/her to copy from a peer or have the peer write the directions.

339. Accompany written directions with a visual demonstration or model whenever possible.

340. Always have the student read written directions at least two times. Allow the student extra time to underline or highlight key words and phrases.

341. When there are multiple written directions on an assignment, have the student place a colored dot between each segment of the instruction.

342. Always check for understanding before the student begins the assignment.

343. For visually impaired students always give test directions, assignments and important directions orally.

344. Place a piece of yellow acetate over the page of print to enhance the contrast and darken the print for student's with a visual impairment.

345. Use black flair pens to trace over directions and darken the print for students with low vision.

346. For visually impaired students use a white board with erasable black marker or if available a green chalkboard in place of a blackboard.

Chapter Ten

Large Group Instruction

Oral Presentations

A large portion of the school day is spent listening to the classroom teacher or special education teacher present material orally. A great amount of material presented daily is in lecture format. This can be a frustrating experience for the student who experiences difficulty with auditory processing.

347. Always state goals and objectives of the lesson at the beginning of the session.

348. Review previous lessons, notes and vocabulary so the student is able to build on prior information.

349. Provide information in an organized sequential format.

350. Present only the relevant information. Use nouns when possible. The use of pronouns may cause confusion to some students, especially if they did not understand the subject at the beginning of the lecture.

351. Simplify the vocabulary, especially when the student is required to take notes.

352. When giving oral presentations, provide visual aids for the student. Use the overhead, the blackboard, charts or provide visual demonstrations to increase the understanding of subject material.

353. Pause frequently when giving an oral presentation. Ask the student to summarize information. Ask questions to check for understanding and relate information to previously learned concepts as much as possible.

354. Make sure the student removes all unnecessary materials from the desk. During oral presentations the student should have two sharpened pencils, paper and a highlighter on top of the desk.

355. Vary the level of questioning during the classroom discussions so all students will be able to participate.

Note Taking Skills

Note taking is a difficult process. Think about the last time you attended a class or a workshop and needed to take notes. Did you take notes on the syllabus provided for you? Perhaps you brought a tape player from home and recorded the information so you could listen to it in your car on the way home. Did you jot down key words and phrases? Or did you write entire phrases verbatim? Perhaps you were able to generalize the information and fill in a chart or a graph. When the presenter stated, "This is important!" Did you furiously try to write every word? As adults we use many different strategies at different times and in different situations. Note taking is not a simple skill. It requires the student to process information auditory and visually. The student must be able to output the information in another format. In this case, a written format. Students must be taught various strategies to take notes successfully.

356. Encourage the student to take notes in their own words.

357. Teach students to use abbreviations during note taking.

358. Provide the student with an outline of the main topics you will be presenting. Provide space for the student to write notes on the outline sheet.

359. Write major points on the blackboard or overhead so the student is able to copy it.

360. Before the presentation, provide the student with a list of questions for which they will be held responsible to discuss.

361. Cue the student to the major points with the use of key phrases, such as please remember this, this point is very important, or write this down, while the student is taking notes.

362. When comparing and contrasting information, provide the student with graphs or charts to complete.

363. Teach the student to use a time line when information is presented in chronological order.

364. Teach the student to jot down key words if there is not enough time to complete the thought.

365. If you are providing a visual demonstration, allow the student sufficient time to copy material into the notes.

366. If the student is unable to take notes, allow a peer to use carbon paper or make a photocopy of his/her notes. The student should still take notes during the presentation to practice the skill and be an active participant.

367. Allow time at the end of each oral presentation for the students to compare and discuss their notes.

368. Summarize important points at the end of the presentation. Teach the students highlight important information in their notes.

369. When using an overhead machine with transparencies, allow the student with low vision to look directly into the overhead projector while the transparency is projected onto the wall.

370. An overhead projector will assist the student with a hearing impairment. It will allow the student to see the presentation and read the teacher's lips simultaneously.

371. Create an audiocassette of the presentation. Allow the student to take it home.

Chapter Eleven

Classroom Assessments

Many students with special needs require alternate forms of assessment due to difficulties with reading and written language. Always keep in mind what type of information you would like to gain from the assessment. If the goal is to measure the student's knowledge of a curriculum area, it is important to test only the curriculum area and not to penalize the student for his/her disability.

372. Allow the student to test orally with a peer, the classroom teacher, special education teacher or inclusion assistant.

373. Allow the student to demonstrate the concept or the process or to illustrate what she/he has learned.

374. Write the answers to the questions for the student. Be sure to record the answers verbatim.

375. Allow the student extra time to complete the test.

376. Read all test directions orally.

377. When administering final grades, make sure you are aware of the mastery criteria on the Individualized Educational Plan.

378. Tape record the test and allow students to tape record their answers.

379. If the test permits, allow students to respond only to the even or odd numbered problems.

380. Maintain a record of the pretests and posttests. Grade on individual progress and improvement.

381. Limit the number of concepts presented on each test.

382. Divide the test into segments. Each segment should have only one set of directions.

383. Test frequently to monitor progress. Use daily quizzes.

384. Circle, underline or have the students highlight key words.

385. Allow students to test individually with the special education teacher or inclusion assistant.

386. Use recognition of facts rather than factual recall on tests. Delete the trick questions on commercially made tests.

387. If the district requires the student to take standardized tests, order consumable tests. This will eliminate the need for the student to transfer the response to a computer score sheet.

388. Most standardized tests rely heavily on the student's ability to read the material. If the student's reading level is several years below grade level, this may be a frustrating experience. Address this issue during the IEP meeting. If the student does not participate in standardized testing, it must be addressed in the Individual Education Plan.

389. If the student takes the standardized tests, compare the results to the individualized testing records in the special education folder. If results on standardized testing are discrepant, place a label on testing data stating that the test

scores are invalid. Individual ability and achievement scores are listed in the Individual Education Plan.

Teacher Made Tests

Formal and informal assessments occur daily in the classroom setting. When creating teacher made, curriculum based assessments use the following guidelines.

390. Write directions in a clear, precise format.

391. Include one direction per sentence.

392. Underline or box the directions. This will help to separate the information from the remainder of the text.

393. Provide examples of correct responses. This will act as a visual aid for the student.

394. Use large bold print whenever possible.

395. Leave ample space between problems. Avoid making tests that have a cluttered appearance.

396. Avoid using words such as never, not, sometimes and always.

397. When creating multiple choice tests, exclude statements such as *all of the above* or *none of the above*.

398. When creating matching tests, organize both columns so the students' choices are clear and concise.

399. When creating true and false tests, eliminate words such as *all* or *never*. Avoid using double negatives that may be misinterpreted.

400. Create fill in the blank tests, by placing the choices under the blank space instead of at the end of the sentence.

401. When giving essay tests, provide the student with a blank outline format, so the student may organize ideas before beginning to write.

402. Allow students to keep a portfolio of work samples. The students should place their best work in the portfolio. This may be used as an alternate form of assessment.

403. Allow the student to demonstrate the knowledge learned by creating a project or demonstrating key concepts.

404. Allow the student to create an audio or videocassette demonstrating knowledge of the content area.

Alternate Grading Systems

Several grading alternatives may be considered for students with special needs. Many educators use a traditional percentage grading system. This system may not be appropriate for students in an inclusion classroom.

405. The IEP will provide the frame work for grading the student with a disability.

406. Effort and performance should be considered when determining the student's grades.

407. Contract grading is often used in inclusionary settings. The student and teacher determine the quantity and quality of

work that the student must complete in order to receive a specific grade in a subject area.

408. Combination grading can reward students for their performance and help to individualize the grading process. In this manner, the student is graded on their ability, effort and achievement. The ability grade is based on the expected amount of improvement in the subject area. The effort grade is based on the amount of time and effort the student put into the assignment to master the concept. The achievement grade is related to the student's mastery in relation to others in the class. The three grades can be averaged together into one grade.

409. Shared grading is frequently used in inclusionary settings. With shared grading the regular and the special education teacher collaborate to assign grades to students. The final grade is based on the grades and observations of both teachers.

410. A pass/fail grading system may be appropriate. This system acknowledges that the student has completed the required assignments as determined by the teachers and the IEP.

411. If the report card does not correspond with the student's individual goals and objectives on the IEP, write descriptive comments. List the skills that have been mastered. Include this letter with the student's report card.

Chapter Twelve

Attention Deficit Disorder

"I just don't know what to do anymore! The student is always out of his seat or walking around the room!" "The student is so disruptive in the classroom that it is affecting the other students." "The student seems to be in a dreamland. Even though the student is looking at me, she doesn't seem to be able to focus on what I am saying or follow through on the assignments." These are common concerns heard regularly by professionals and parents. Each year many students with disabilities are also medically diagnosed as ADD. Modifications will need to be made for these students within the classroom setting if the student is to experience success in school. If a student is diagnosed as ADD and is on medication, it is important to obtain a release of information from the parent and talk directly with the doctor or psychologist. Also, meet with the parents. They will be able to provide valuable information to you about their child. Adapt the strategies that have worked at home into the classroom setting if possible. For the majority of the students, the strategies and modifications discussed previously in this book will assist the student in achieving success in the classroom. The strategies in this section pertain directly to the student who experiences difficulty with attention, on task behavior, impulsivity, and distractibility.

Structuring the Environment

Daily structure needs to be provided for all students, but for these students it is especially important. Transition times are difficult and should be closely monitored.

412. Keep a daily schedule on the board. Discuss the schedule and point out any changes that will occur in advance.

413. Provide extra structure during transition times. Allow the student time to adjust and organize their materials before beginning a new subject.

414. Review the classroom rules frequently. If a student is having difficulty with a specific rule, write down the rule for the student. Be clear and concise. Give the student specific examples of the rule.

415. Always state what the student should do, instead of what the student should not do. If the student is running in the hall, simply say, "Walk, please."

416. Try to schedule the strong academic areas in the morning.

417. Check-in and check-out times are important for the student. Enlist the support of the special education teacher or inclusion assistant if the student has special needs. If not, obtain the support of the school social worker or counselor.

418. Assist the student with a homework notebook. If a telephone is available, allow the student to call and leave a message for him/herself.

419. A three-ring notebook with pocket folders will help the student to keep all supplies, materials and assignments in one place. Instruct the student never to remove an assignment unless it is time to turn it in to the teacher.

420. Allow the student to check out an extra copy of all of the textbooks for home use.

Behavior and Attention Difficulties

421. Make sure you have the student's attention when talking to him or her. Eye contact is important.

422. Provide small group instruction as much as possible.

423. Give one or two step directions. Check for understanding of each direction.

424. Give only one assignment at a time.

425. Allow ample time for hands-on instruction. This will help actively engage the student in the learning process. Active participation is extremely important for this student. It will assist the student in remaining focused.

426. Modify daily assignments to alleviate frustration. (See the section on Modification of Daily Assignments).

427. Use computer instruction for academic reinforcement if appropriate. This allows the student to receive immediate feedback, it allows the student to self-pace the instruction and may help to increase motivation.

428. Use a timer to assist the student in remaining focused. Set the timer to coincide with the amount of time you perceive the student is able to remain focused. Tell the student what you expect him/her to complete during the allotted time. Gradually increase the time.

429. Allow the student time during the day to get up, walk around and stretch. Give the student clear guidelines about which times are appropriate.

430. Use random strategies when calling on students in the classroom. Place the students' names in a basket and draw the name randomly. Since the students do not know who will be called on next, attention increases.

431. Provide forms of immediate feedback for the student. Provide self-correctors for the student's assignments. Many student's will benefit from the immediate feedback.

Impulsivity and Distractibility

"She just doesn't think!" "He always blurts out the answer before he is called on!" Do one or two students come to mind when you hear these questions? Many students tend to act before thinking. Impulsive students may also be easily distracted.

432. Place creative artwork in the back of the classroom to eliminate visual distractions for the student. Avoid excessive materials that may distract the student.

433. Check the seating arrangements. Students who are easily distracted should not be seated near doors, windows or high traffic areas.

434. For the easily distracted student allow extra time to complete assignments, even when the assignments have been modified.

435. Avoid timed activities and tests. Many students become frustrated when they notice other students have completed the assignment. The student will either guess or give up on the assignment.

436. Teach the student to stop and think before responding. Create a visual signal between the adult and student. An example of a visual signal would be to place your finger aside your nose. When the student observes this, he/she will know that it is time to slow down and think about the action.

437. Teach the student to talk to himself/herself. This is commonly referred to as self-talk. This is especially helpful with complex steps and directions. It will also assist the student in remaining focused on the current task.

438. Assign the student to a special seat. Seat the student near students who are quiet, independent workers. Provide good role models. Do not seat disruptive or students that are easily distracted together.

439. Allow the student to have only the necessary materials for the current assignment on top of the desk. Toys and play objects should remain at home.

Reinforcement and Discipline

Many students with disabilities who are medically diagnosed as ADD may be more dependent on external reinforcement than other students in the classroom. In an inclusion setting, these students may need constant reassurance they are doing well. A reward system may meet this need. Other areas reward systems are frequently used may include the cafeteria, study period, or during recess.

440. If the student consistently needs to be disciplined during a specific academic area, it is important to check to see if the current modifications are appropriate.

441. Use a reward system. Since the student will need continuous and frequent feedback, break the educational day into

time blocks. Some students may need feedback every five to ten minutes at the initiation of the program. This can easily be done by placing a chart on the students desk and placing a check or a sticker onto the chart or index card as you walk around the room. Gradually increase time to cover the academic subject block.

442. The class discipline plan may not always be an appropriate plan for the student. The student may need a supplemental discipline plan with extra warnings, coupled with a reward system.

443. A token system works well for the student. This is an easy method. Keep a pocketful of tokens. The tokens may consist of small laminated paper shapes, buttons, beads, or pennies. You may choose to make your own. In this manner the student keeps the tokens in a container in their desk and turns in the appropriate number for a reward. Most students at the beginning will work for the easy rewards. When using tokens they will have an option to save the tokens for a larger reward.

444. With the student, create a list of reinforcement activities. The student may choose from these activities when the goal has been met. What may seem like a motivator to you, may not be a motivator for the student. Create the list together and keep the rewards simple. Some easy suggestions may include stickers, pencils, pens, basic school supplies, ten extra minutes on the computer, a can of pop, ten minutes of free choice activity with a friend, a coupon for one excused homework assignment or daily assignment.

445. An inexpensive way to purchase trinkets for younger students is to attend garage sales during the summer. There are many small items that may be purchased for five cents or less. Many teachers have created form letters to send to various large companies. Many companies have promotional items they will send to you free of charge if you are an educator.

446. Keep the parents informed when the student has shown improvement during the day. Create a list of positive sayings such as:

Awesome Day!
I discovered the secret to success today!
Super Star!
I'm a Great Student!
Wow!

Photocopy these sayings onto fluorescent paper. Cut into strips. Place these strips into an envelope. If the student has had a good day, he or she may choose a strip to take home. If proper guidelines are set, the older student will be able to monitor his or her own progress. This may also be an indicator to the parents that the student had a great day.

447. Inform the parents about the reward system you are using. Most parents will provide reinforcement in the home also. Coordinate a communication system between the school and home.

448. A daily report can also be used to monitor behavior and academic goals. An easy way to create a daily report is to tape an index card to the student's desk. Subjects can be added to the card as they are presented during the day. For younger students a happy face may be placed on the card after the subject if the student has experienced success during the time block. For older students a rating scale of 1-5 may be used. This report may be sent home daily to increase communication between the school and the home.

449. A daily log has proven successful in coordinating home and school communication. Both parents and teachers can use this log to write comments, concerns and suggestions for and about the student. The student is rewarded for remembering to take home and return the notebook on a daily basis.

450. Teach the student to use positive self talk. "I can do this!" "I can handle this!" or "I'm good at this!" are all examples

of self-talk. If you hear a student using negative self-talk or putting him or herself down, stop the student and help the student to rephrase the comments positively.

Afterword

People learn in many different ways. Some people learn through observation. Others learn by reading and studying. Still others learn through doing. Nowhere has it ever been stated that inclusion will be easy. You will encounter roadblocks while setting up your inclusion program. You also will discover workable solutions. You will make mistakes and you will learn a great deal from trial and error. I hope, though, with the use of this book, the transition will be smooth and the modifications will be easier to make.

You have taken the first step. You have read this book. Now it is up to you to take the next step. I encourage you to take it. The next step will make a change in the lives of many children. It is the students' right to belong in the classroom. It is our job, as educators, to provide the most appropriate program within the least restrictive environment.

Write to me and let me know about your experiences! As you set up your program, use this manual. Write down the ideas that have worked well for you! As you make your modifications, note in the book the ones that have worked exceptionally well for you. Add your own ideas to the lists. If you have new ideas, tips, comments or suggestions for the revised edition, let me know. Good luck!

Ω

Appendix

Developing An Inclusion Program Checklist

❐ List the benefits and possible barriers of an inclusion program in your school. Worksheet 3.

❐ Target a specific grade level in which to develop your program.
_____Grade level
_____Number of students

❐ Fill out the information on the Student Data Sheet. Worksheet 5.

❐ Group the students. Worksheet 7.

❐ Determine the number of assistants and the total number of assistant hours you will need to implement the program. Worksheet 8.

❐ Create an outline of a tentative schedule. Worksheet 10.

❐ Present the plan! Worksheet 11.

❐ Survey the staff for in-service needs. Worksheet 12.

❐ Discuss classroom set up and teaching styles with the volunteer inclusion teachers. Worksheet 13.

❐ Use the follow-up surveys to determine program needs.
Student Survey-Worksheet 14
Parent Survey-Worksheet 15
Inclusion Assistant Survey-Worksheet 16
Staff Survey-Worksheet 17

Benefits and Barriers
Example

(Use the blank form on the reverse side to write the benefits and possible barriers you may encounter in your school. These ideas will get you started.)

Benefits of Inclusion
* Students receive service with their peers to the greatest possible extent.
* Students no longer are labeled by their peers because they leave the classroom to attend a special class.
* Students can participate in all instructional activities with proper modifications, even though the outcome may be different.
* Students do not lose valuable academic learning time transitioning between regular education and special education classrooms.
* Students no longer need to work within two fragmented educational systems.
* Students are not pulled in so many directions. All related services are provided within the classroom setting.
* The special education teacher develops a better understanding of the classroom curriculum. Modification strategies that work for the student in one academic area, may be transferred to other academic areas.
* Students become more accepting of one another regardless of the disability.
* The special education teacher or inclusion assistant is able to assist other students within the classroom setting if needed.
* Communication between regular education and special education increases.
* Classroom teachers have more flexibility. They do not have to wait for students to return from their special class in order to begin a new lesson.

Possible Barriers
* Scheduling difficulties.
* Grouping of students.

Inclusion:
Benefits and Possible Barriers

Benefits:

Barriers:

Student Data Sheet Example

	Student's Name	Disability	Assistant Time	Reading	Written Language	Math	Social/ Emotional	Speech/ Language	OT/PT DAPE	Other
1	Mary	LD		300	150	300			OT 60	
2	John	MMI	1500	300	300	300		90	DAPE 60	
3	Lynn	LD		150	150					
4	Jake	LD				300		60		
5	Joey	LD		300						
6	Heidi	OHI	600	300	300	300		90	OT 60 PT 60	Health 300
7	Amy	LD		300						
8	Mike	LD		300						
9	Steve	BD	300				300			
10	Frank	VI	300	300	150					Enlargement 60
11	James	LD			300				OT 60	
12	Alicia	LD				300			OT 60	
13	Mark	BD					300			
14	Tim	LD		300	300	300		90		

Minutes of Service in Accordance with the Students Individualized Education Plan

Student Data Sheet

Student's Name	Disability	Assistant Time	Reading	Written Language	Math	Social/ Emotional	Speech/ Language	OT/PT DAPE	Other
1									
2									
3									
4									
5									
6									
7									
8									
9									
10									
11									
12									
13									
14									

Minutes of Service in Accordance with the Students Individualized Education Plan

Student Groupings
Example

Use this form as a worksheet to assist you with grouping of students. Group students into the fewest number of classrooms possible, preferably four or five students per classroom. Make several copies of Worksheet 7 and experiment with various different groupings.

GIVEN THE HYPOTHETICAL GROUPS ON WORKSHEET #3 THE STUDENTS WERE GROUPED IN THE FOLLOWING WAY.

Classroom #1   Approximate level _____

❏ Consultation   ❏ Special Education Assistant   ❏ Special Education Teacher
                 (2 hours per day)   (consultation only)

      1. Lynn - LD   2. Brandon - LD   3. Steve - BD   4. Paul - LD   5. Aaron - HI

(One possible reason for this grouping is that the students receive minimal amount of academic service. All of the students should be able to receive their direct instruction from the classroom teacher. Steve has a pupil assistant written into his IEP for approximately 1 hour per day. This assistant could help to support the other four students during this time. A program assistant would be beneficial for one hour per day to assist the group with reading and written language. This inclusion assistant would be scheduled at a different time than the BD pupil assistant to provide extended coverage for all. Brandon receives service for language. If the language service is incorporated into the classroom, the teacher would be able to support the other students with curriculum vocabulary also.)

Classroom #2   Approximate level _____

❏ Consultation   ❏ Special Education Assistant   ❏ Special Education Teacher
                 (2 hours per day)   (1 - 2 hours per day. Includes related
                                                      support services.)

      1. Heidi - OHI   2. Joey - LD   3. Mary - LD   4. Mike - LD   5. Amy - LD

(This group of students receives a greater amount of service than the previous group. Three of the students receive service for reading only. Heidi and Mary have the greatest academic needs. Heidi has a pupil assistant assigned to her for two hours per day. This person will be able to support Heidi along with the students who need reading support. In this classroom the students also receive support for occupational therapy and physical therapy. The occupational therapy could be incorporated into the written language block, so assistance may be provided to others if needed. A special education teacher will need to provide direct service for instruction in this classroom.)

Classroom #3   Approximate level _____
☐ Consultation   ☐ Special Education Assistant   ☐ Special Education Teacher
                  (Full time pupil support)   (1-2 hours per day including related
                                                             support)

            1. Frank - VI   2. Mark - BD   3. John - MMI

(In this group, John has a full time assistant assigned to him. Mark was placed in this group so his behavior goals may be monitored throughout the day. Frank will need many modifications due to his visual impairment. This is the only class that has a full time assistant. It would be appropriate to place these three students in the same classroom. Due to the special requirements the special education teacher should be involved on a daily basis. These students do receive related services. The inclusion pupil assistant will need to take break or have lunch when a related support person is able to support the classroom.)

Classroom #4   Approximate level _____
☐ Consultation   ☐ Special Education Assistant   ☐ Special Education Teacher
                                                  (1 hour plus related services)

            1. Tim - LD   2. Jake - LD   3. James - LD   4. Alicia - LD

(In this group the service will vary. Several of the students receive OT services, speech and language, and will also need support in academic areas. There is no pupil assistant assigned to this group so you would try to incorporate the related services into the curriculum as much as possible.)

These groups could be changed in many ways. Since three of the classrooms in this hypothetical situation have pupil support assistants, the students could possibly be grouped into three classrooms and the inclusion support could be redistributed, allowing for maximum coverage throughout the day. The students could be grouped by services received or math skills. The grouping and scheduling process will take time. Always keep in mind that no matter how many times you group and regroup the students, you will never find a perfect group. You will find a group you feel will be manageable.

<u>Student Groupings</u>

Use this form as a worksheet to guide you with student groups. Group the students into the fewest number of classrooms possible. You will need several copies of this worksheet. Experiment with various groups.

Classroom #1   Approximate level _____
❏ Consultation   ❏Special Education Assistant   ❏ Special Education Teacher

Classroom #2   Approximate level _____
❏ Consultation   ❏Special Education Assistant   ❏ Special Education Teacher

Student Groupings

Classroom #3   Approximate level _____
☐ Consultation   ☐ Special Education Assistant   ☐ Special Education Teacher

Classroom #4   Approximate level _____
☐ Consultation   ☐ Special Education Assistant   ☐ Special Education Teacher

Learning Styles
(Group students with similar learning styles into classrooms)

Math and Problem Solving Skills

Low   **Average**   **High**

Related Services

Speech/Language Services	Occupational Therapy	Adaptive Physical Education	Other Related Services

Classroom #1	Classroom #2	Classroom #3	Classroom #4

Assistant Minutes

(Calculate the amount of assistant time as carefully as possible, with the information you currently have. Build 15 minutes of daily consultation time into the schedule.)

Classroom #1
Pupil Inclusion Assistant
(assigned to a specific student)
Student contact time: _____
Consultation time: _____
Lunch: _____
Break: _____

Inclusion Program Assistant
(assigned to a classroom of students)
Student contact time: _____
Consultation time: _____
Lunch: _____
Break: _____

Total Minutes: _____

Classroom #2
Pupil Inclusion Assistant
(assigned to a specific student)
Student contact time: _____
Consultation time: _____
Lunch: _____
Break: _____

Inclusion Program Assistant
(assigned to a classroom of students)
Student contact time: _____
Consultation time: _____
Lunch: _____
Break: _____

Total Minutes: _____

Assistant Minutes

Classroom #3

Pupil Inclusion Assistant
(assigned to a specific student)
Student contact time: _____
Consultation time: _____
Lunch: _____
Break: _____

Inclusion Program Assistant
(assigned to a classroom of students)
Student contact time: _____
Consultation time: _____
Lunch: _____
Break: _____

Total Minutes: _____

Classroom #4

Pupil Inclusion Assistant
(assigned to a specific student)
Student contact time: _____
Consultation time: _____
Lunch: _____
Break: _____

Inclusion Program Assistant
(assigned to a classroom of students)
Student contact time: _____
Consultation time: _____
Lunch: _____
Break: _____

Total Minutes: _____

Sample Schedule for an Inclusion Setting

This is a schedule currently used in an inclusion setting. The students are grouped by reading abilities. There are 17 students in this inclusion program. The program is serviced by one full time special education teacher and an inclusion assistant who is employed three hours per day. There are no students in this program that have a full time inclusion assistant.

Daily Schedule

| 8:00 - 9:00 | Preparation, communication and planning time |
| 9:00 - 9:30 | Communication time with classroom teachers. (Changes in daily lesson plans. Overview of daily schedule. Sign up for flexible time). |

Morning Block

Classroom #1 4 Students	Classroom #2 4 Students	Classroom #3 5 students	Classroom #4 4 Students
9:40 - 11:15 Reading and language arts block with the **special education teacher.** Supplemental curriculum provided by the special education department when classroom assignments are not appropriate or cannot be modified.	**9:40 - 11:15** Social Studies and Science block. Movies, large group instruction story, break. Activities that do not require the assistance of the special education department	**9:40-11:15** Reading and language arts block with the **inclusion assistant.** Reteaching, modification to the curriculum and support. Direct instruction is provided by theclassroom teacher.	**9:40 - 10:40** Specials: Music, gym, art, technology, and media. - - - - - - - - - - - - - - - **10:40-11:15** Large group instruction, spelling, break. Activity that does not require the assistance of the special education department.

| **11:15 - 12:00** Specials: Music, gym, art, technology, and media. - - - - - - - - - - - - - - **12:00 - 12:30** Handwriting, spelling practice, get ready for lunch. No special education support is provided during this block. | **11:15-12:20** Reading and language arts block with the **special education teacher.** Supplemental curriculum provided by the special education department when classroom assignments arenot appropriate. | **11:15 - 12:20** Movies, large group instruction, story, and break. Activities that do not require the assistance of the special education department | **11:15-12:30** Reading and language arts block with the **inclusion assistant.** Reteaching, modification to the curriculum and support. Direct instruction is provided by the classroom teacher. |

Sample Schedule for an Inclusion Setting

12:30 - 1:00
Lunch for the classroom teachers, special education teacher and inclusion assistant

Afternoon Block

1:00 - 2:15 Social Studies/Science large group activities. - - - - - - - - - - - - - - - **1:00 - 1:45** **Special education teacher is available during this time** on a sign up basis. This should be done 1-2 days in advance.	**1:00 - 1:45** Specials: Music, gym, art, technology, and media. - - - - - - - - - - - - - - - **1:45 - 2:15** **Special education teacher is** available on a sign up basis.	**1:00 - 1:45** Specials: Music, gym, art, technology, and media. - - - - - - - - - - - - - - - **1:45 - 2:15** **Special education teacher available** on a sign up basis.	**1:00 - 2:15** Social Studies/Science large group activities. - - - - - - - - - - - - - - - **1:00 - 1:45** **Special education teacher available.** Sign up basis.

1:00 - 2:15 This time block is considered "flexible time" for the special education teacher. The classroom teachers should let you know in advance if you will be needed. A sign up sheet should be provided to the classroom teachers.	This time block will allow you to provide support across the curriculum for the students.	**Suggestions** for this time block may include: - Alternate forms of testing for spelling, math, social studies and science. - Team teaching or support for social studies and science activities may be incorporated.	- Drill and practice activities that support the curriculum. - Planning time and consultation with classroom teachers that have preparation time during this time block. - An assistant available during this time will increase the flexibility.

2:35 - 3:35 Math
In this schedule the students are grouped for math. All students that are on an Individualized Education are grouped into one classroom. In this sample schedule there are 7 students who received math services. The math block is team taught on a daily basis.

3:35 - 3:50
Check outs and homework assignments are monitored during this time.

Preliminary Schedule Worksheet

Daily Schedule

Notes:_____

_____

_____

Morning Block

Classroom #1 __ Students	Classroom #2 __ Students	Classroom #3 __ Students	Classroom #4 __ Students
Time _____	Time _____	Time _____	Time _____
Time _____	Time _____	Time _____	Time _____
Time _____	Time _____	Time _____	Time _____
Time _____	Time _____	Time _____	Time _____

Preliminary Schedule Worksheet

Daily Schedule

Notes:_____

_____

_____

Afternoon Block

Classroom #1 __ Students	Classroom #2 __ Students	Classroom #3 __ Students	Classroom #4 __ Students
Time _____	Time _____	Time _____	Time _____
Time _____	Time _____	Time _____	Time _____
Time _____	Time _____	Time _____	Time _____
Time _____	Time _____	Time _____	Time _____

Presenting the Plan

Place the following materials into an information packet:

* A brief written summary of your proposal.

* The list of advantages and possible barriers of inclusion. Worksheet 3.

* A list of the target group of students and the grade level information.

* A copy of the student data sheet. Worksheet 5.

* An approximate calculation of the number of assistants and the hours you will need. Worksheet 8.

* Tentative schedule outlines. Worksheet 10.

* Other data you have collected that will support the program.

Staff Survey
In-service Needs

The following survey will assist the Special Education Department in determining the needs of the building staff in relation to inclusion.

	Disagree				Agree

1. I understand the concept of inclusion. 1 2 3 4 5

2. I am willing to participate in an inclusion program. 1 2 3 4 5

3. I am willing to accept a group of students with disabilities into my classroom. 1 2 3 4 5

4. I will need training and in-service before I would be willing to accept a group of students with disabilities into the classroom. 1 2 3 4 5

5. I would like to receive in-service in the following areas. (Please check all that apply.)

What is inclusion? ☐
Collaboration Skills ☐
Modifying the Curriculum ☐
Working Effectively with
   Inclusion Assistants ☐
Support Services and
   Resources. ☐
Other: (Please write below). ☐

_____
_____
_____
_____

Please write any comments or suggestions and return this survey to me. Thank you very much.

Classroom Setup Checklist
(Use the following questions as guidelines.)

Planning. What time of day would be best to meet informally? When planning larger units or lessons, when would be a good time to meet? Who will take responsibility for planning?

Lesson format. How will the lessons be taught? Who will take responsibility for daily planning? What type of teaching system will work for all involved? How will the lessons be presented and by whom?

Responsibility. Who will be responsible for the students' grades? What grading system will be used? How will the modifications affect the grade? Who will be responsible to make the modifications and to hold the student accountable for classroom assignments?

Classroom routines. What are the classroom routines? Pencil sharpening? Bathroom breaks? Turning in assignments?

Classroom discipline. Who will be responsible for classroom discipline? What is the discipline plan? Will all students use the same discipline plan? What are the rewards and consequences?

Additional comments or concerns that should be addressed:

Student Survey

1. **How do you feel about your new class placement?**

2. **How do you feel you are performing in the classroom?**

3. **Are you following the classroom rules?**

4. **Are the academic modifications to the curriculum helping you?**

5. **Are you receiving enough support in the classroom?**

6. **Are you able to complete the classwork and the homework assignments?**

7. **How do you get along with the other students in your classroom?**

8. **Are you involved in extracurricular activities? If the answer is no, what type of extracurricular activities would you be interested in joining?**

_____
Signature/Date

Parent Survey

1. What are your reactions and feelings to your child's new placement?

2. How does your child feel about the new placement?

3. How is your child coping with the new academic demands of the classroom setting?

4. How would you rate your child's self esteem in the new setting?

5. How do you feel your child interacts with his/her peers?

6. Have you noticed any changes (positive or negative) in your child since his/her new placement?

7. Can you suggest any ideas or strategies that may assist us in working with your child?

Additional Comments:

_____

Signature/Date

Inclusion Assistant Survey

1. How do you feel the students are performing in the classroom?

2. Do you have any specific concerns about the students?

<u>Student's Name</u>   <u>Area of Concern</u>

3. Do you feel you receive sufficient guidance from the Special Services department? If not, please list suggestions for improvement.

4. Do you feel you have adequate time to communicate with the classroom teachers with which you are directly involved with?

5. Do you have suggestions for specific modifications or adaptations to the curriculum?

6. What types of inservice or training do you feel would be beneficial for you as an inclusion assistant?

Additional comments, questions or concerns that should be addressed:

_____

Signature / Date

Staff Survey

1. How are the students performing in your classroom?
   Academically- (If a student is experiencing difficulty, indicate the student and the specific areas.)

   Social/ Emotional-(How are the students interacting with their peers?)

2. Are the students completing daily classwork and homework assignments?

3. How are the students' work habits and study skills?

4. How do the students respond to the classroom behavior management system?

5. How do you feel the placement has affected the students' self esteem?

6. How is the communication system working for you?

7. In general, are you satisfied with the students' progress in your classroom? Are you comfortable with the number of students in your classroom?

8. What solutions would you have to any of the problem areas mentioned above?

9. What changes would you like to see in the program?

Additional Comments:

_____
Signature/date

Curriculum Modifications
Student Worksheet

Student's Name:_____ Grade _____ Date _____

Team Members:_____

Step 1: List the students strengths.
_____
_____
_____

Step 2: List the goals.
_____
_____
_____

Step 3: Ideas and Strategies for Modifications.

Textbook Modifications:
_____
_____
_____

Daily Assignments:
_____
_____
_____

Written Language:
_____
_____
_____

Spelling:
_____
_____
_____
_____

Mathematics:

_____
_____
_____
_____

Organizational Skills:

_____
_____
_____

Directions:

_____
_____
_____

Large Group Instruction:

_____
_____
_____

Classroom Assessments:

_____
_____
_____

Classroom Behavior:

_____
_____
_____

Other areas of concern:

_____
_____
_____

*Person responsible for the modifications:

Textbook:_____   Daily Assignments:_____

Written Language:_____   Spelling:_____

Mathematics:_____   Organizational Skills:_____

Directions:_____   Group Instruction: _____

Assessments:_____   Behavior:_____

Other:_____

*Special education teacher, classroom teacher, inclusion assistant, peers, volunteers, related service personnel (OT, PT, DAPE), other school personnel - e.g. art, physical education, technology, music, or media specialists.

Overview of
Curriculum Modifications

Student's name:_____ Date:_____

Homeroom teacher:_____

Special Education teacher:_____

Note the modifications that will need to be made for the student in the following areas. Fill in the name of the person responsible for the modifications. Make copies and distribute to all team members. If no modifications are needed at the present time, leave the area blank. Modifications may be added at a later date.

Textbook / Person Responsible:
_____
_____
_____
_____

Daily Assignments / Person Responsible:
_____
_____
_____
_____

Written Language / Person Responsible:
_____
_____
_____
_____

Spelling / Person Responsible

_____
_____
_____
_____

Math / Person Responsible:

_____
_____
_____
_____

Directions (Oral and Written) / Person Responsible:

_____
_____
_____
_____

Testing Procedures / Person Responsible:

_____
_____
_____
_____

Large & Small Group Instructions / Person Responsible:

_____
_____
_____
_____

Organizational Skills / Person Responsible:

_____
_____
_____
_____

Textbook Modifications
Student Worksheet

Student's name: _____ Date of Planning Meeting: _____
Subject:_____ Grade:_____

Team Members
Name: Title:

_____   _____
_____   _____
_____   _____
_____   _____

Please check all modifications that apply to the individual student.

☐ **The student will need assistance with modifications to the classroom textbook.**
     ☐ The student should read all classroom texts with a peer or with a small group.
     ☐ Audiocassettes should be provided to the student.
     ☐ The entire textbook should be provided on audiocassettes.
     ☐ The entire textbook should be paraphrased for the student.
     ☐ Alternating pages of the text should be recorded for the student.
     ☐ _____
*Person responsible for the modifications:_____

☐ **The student will need the following supplemental services.**
     ☐ Preteaching or previewing of the material.
     ☐ Outline of the required text.
     ☐ List of vocabulary words and definitions. A modified list if appropriate.
     ☐ Checklist of required assignments with due dates.
     ☐ Study guide for required assignments.
     ☐ A complete set of textbooks should be provided for home use.
     ☐ _____
*Person responsible for the modifications:_____

☐ **The student will require direct support from the Special Education Department.**
     ☐A supplemental textbook will be needed
        Who will provide the service? _____
        Number of minutes daily? _____
        Time of day service will be needed._____

Modifications for Daily Assignments
Student Worksheet

Student's name: _____   Date of Planning Meeting: _____

Subject:_____   Grade:_____

<u>Team Members</u>

Name: Title:

_____   _____

_____   _____

_____   _____

_____   _____

_____   _____

Please check all modifications that apply to the individual student.

❑ **The student will need assistance with modifications for daily assignments.**

    ❑ The student will be able to complete daily class assignments with the following modifications:

    ❑ Modify the length and grading of the assignment.

    ❑ Allow the student to work in a cooperative groups.

    ❑ Allow the student to complete the assignment orally.

    ❑ Allow a peer to read and write the student's ideas.

    ❑ Allow the student extra time to complete the assignment.

    ❑ _____

    ❑ _____

*Person responsible for the modifications:_____

❑ **The student will need the following supplemental services.**

    ❑ A checklist of assignments and due dates.

    ❑ A complete set of textbooks should be provided for home use.

    ❑ A photocopy or a consumable book.

    ❑ _____

* Person responsible for the modifications:_____

☐ **The student will require direct support from the Special Education Department.**
    ☐ Assignments provided at a lower readability level.
    ☐ Supplemental curriculum or adapted materials will be provided covering the same skill area.
        Amount of service daily? _____
        Approximate time of service?_____
* Person responsible to provide the service:_____

☐ **The student is unable to complete the assignments assigned to the class.**
    ☐ Supplemental assignments will be provided in accordance to the student's Individualized Education Plan.
    ☐ The student has a Special Education Inclusion Assistant written into the Individualized Education Plan.
        Amount of service daily? _____
        Areas of special concern._____
        _____

    ☐ Ideas for supplemental materials. _____
    _____
    _____
    _____

* Person responsible to provide the service:_____

Additional comments:

Glossary

abstract thinking - ability to think in terms of ideas.

ADD - see Attention Deficit Disorder

alternate assessments - an evaluation using various methods in place of traditional paper/pencil tests to assess a student's knowledge. Demonstrations, oral presentations or projects are some examples.

Attention Deficit Disorder - a condition in which a student has difficulties in directing or maintaining attention to normal tasks of learning.

auditory blending - blending of sounds into words.

auditory discrimination - ability to hear differences and similarities in spoken word.

auditory memory - ability to recall information that is heard.

behavior - a relationship between a stimulus and a response.

behavior modification - the process which creates a change in the stimulus/response pattern.

collaboration - to work together towards a common goal.

configuration cues - the outline of a word in relation to the shape and length.

contract - a written agreement between teacher and student that outlines specific behaviors and consequences.

discrimination - ability to differentiate between visual, auditory, tactual, or other sensory stimuli.

distractibility - attention that is easily removed away from the task.

expressive language - vocal, gestures and/or written expression.

fine motor - use of small muscle groups for specific tasks such as handwriting.

hyperactivity - excessive activity in relation to others of the same age and in similar situations.

IEP - See Individualized Education Plan.

Individual Education Plan - an individual program designed for a student who qualifies for special education services.

impulsivity - acting or speaking out without considering the consequences.

inclusion assistant - a person who works with a group of students in an inclusion classroom.

inclusion pupil assistant - a person who is assigned to support a specific student. The assistant is written into the IEP.

inclusive schooling - a school setting in which students receive their educational instruction within the classroom setting for the entire or a substantial portion of their school day.

least restrictive environment - a term requiring that, to the greatest possible extent, students with disabilities are educated with their non-disabled peers.

modifications - adaptations made in the curriculum, presentation method, or the environment to provide support for the individual student

memory - recall of visual, auditory, and or tactile stimuli.

mnemonics - visual or word related aids that facilitate retrieval of information.

parallel activity - An assignment in which the outcome is similar but the materials used to reach the outcome may be entirely different.

previewing - reading, listening to, or viewing the selection before instruction or a test.

readiness - physical, mental and emotional preparedness for a learning activity.

remediation - improvement of basic skills.

short attention span - inability to pay attention to something for a long period of time compared to other of the same age.

supplemental teaching - provisions provided to the student in the form of reteaching, reinforcement and/or alternate curriculum when needed.

supportive teaching - modifications made to the classroom curriculum or the environment by the special education teacher or inclusion assistant which will allow the student to experience success in the mainstream.

sound symbol - relationship between the printed form of a letter and the sound.

team teaching - two teachers working together jointly to develop, plan and teach a lesson.

visual discrimination - ability to perceive likenesses and differences in pictures, words and symbols.

Additional Resources

Organizations

If you have specific questions or need additional information,
the following organizations are excellent resources.

Arc of the United States   500 East Border Street, Suite 300   Arlington, TX   76010
Telephone (817) 261-6003
The Arc works to improve the lives of all children and adults with mental retardation and their families. They provide information and referral about mental retardation, the Arc's programs, and local chapters. They have an extensive publications catalog, which includes facts sheets about specific topics related to mental retardation. Some publications are available in Spanish as well as English. Call for additional information.

Autism Society of America (ASA)
7910 Woodmont Avenue   Bethesda, MD   20814
(800) 328-8476 (301) 657-0869 FAX
This organization provides information and referral services and a fax on demand service. There are over 225 local chapters. With the low cost membership, you receive a bimonthly newsletter. Information packets covering a wide range of topics is available at no charge to members. Call for information.

Center on Human Policy - National Resource Center on Community Integration
Syracuse University   805 South Crouse Avenue   Syracuse, NY 13244-2280
(800) 894-0826   (315) 443-4338 FAX
The Center on Human Policy offers a variety of low-cost information packets on topics such as inclusive education, integrated recreation and supported living. Call for a complete list.

Consortium on Inclusive School Practices – Child and Family Studies Program
Allegheny-Singer Research Institute   320 East North Avenue   Pittsburgh, PA   15212
www.asri.edu/CFSP/brochure/abtcons.htm
The Consortium on Inclusive Schooling Practices publishes a "Catalog of products from Funded Projects" which includes a list of manuals, articles, videotapes, brochures, fact sheets, etc. produced by investigators who have received grants from the US Dept of Education, Office of Special Education and Rehabilitative Services.

ERIC Clearinghouse on Disabilities and Gifted Education (ERIC EC)
Council for Exceptional Children 1920 Association Drive   Reston, VA 20191
(800) 328-0272   (703) 264-9449 TTY
A federally funded clearinghouse which focuses on professional literature, information, and resources related to the education and development of those who have disabilities or are gifted. The clearinghouse provides access to the ERIC database with 60,000 citations on disabilities or gifted issues. Many materials are available online at www.cec.sped.org /ericec.htm. The site also offers access to the "Ask ERIC Question-Answering Service" which allows parents and professionals to ask ERIC staff questions about special education.

Institute on Community Integration - University of Minnesota
109 Pattee Hall   150 Pillsbury Dr. SE   Minneapolis, MN   55455
(612) 624-4512   (612) 624-9344 FAX
The Institute has many inexpensive publications and resource guides related to self-advocacy, inclusion, transition, and also curricula for teachers and for paraprofessionals to help in the development of inclusive classrooms. Call for a publications catalog and a complimentary issue of the *Impact* newsletter.

Learning Disabilities Association of America
4156 Library Road   Pittsburgh, PA   15234
(412) 341-1515   (412) 344-0224 FAX
Learning Disabilities Association of America is a nonprofit national organization which provides public awareness, research, and information about learning disabilities. LDA distributes many booklets and books for parents, children and teachers. Call to request a catalog.

National Information Center for Children and Youth with Disabilities (NICHCY)
PO Box 1492   Washington, DC   20013-1492
(800) 695-0285   (202) 884-8441 FAX
NICHCY is an excellent clearinghouse with information on disabilities and disability-related issues, with an emphasis on children and young people birth to age 22. NICHCY will help with personal questions on disabilities; referrals to organizations and agencies; database searches; technical assistance to parent and professional groups.   NICHCY produces many publications. Some may be downloaded free of charge. Many are available in print format for a small fee. Visit the web site at www.nichcy.org.

National Library Service for the Blind and Physically Handicapped
Library of Congress   1291 Taylor Street NW   Washington, DC   20542
(800) 424-8567
The National Library Service distributes reading materials in alternate formats (braille, audiotape) to US citizens who are blind or have a physical impairment that prevents them from using ordinary printed materials.

National Organization for Rare Disorders (NORD)
PO Box 8923   New Fairfield, CT   06182-8923
(203) 746-6518   (203) 746-6481 FAX
NORD is a clearinghouse for more than 5000 rare disorders. The also have a web page with many links to other sources of information. If you are looking for information about a rare disorder this is an excellent place to begin. Call for further information.

PACER Center
4826 Chicago Avenue South   Minneapolis, MN   55417-1098
(612) 827-2966   (612) 827-3065 FAX
PACER stands for the Parent Advocacy Coalition for Educational Rights. PACER is a great organization which helps parents understand special education laws. They have several publications and newsletters which are of interest to parents.

United Cerebral Palsy (UCP)
1600 L Street, NW   Suite 700   Washington, DC   20036
(800) 872-5827   (202) 776-0414 FAX
UCP provides information and referral services. A catalog of publications of interest to parents and advocates is available. Many publications can be downloaded from the website at www.ucpa.org

EXCEPTIONAL RESOURCES AND TRAINING TOOLS
FOR INCLUSIVE EDUCATION

ANTS IN HIS PANTS: Absurdities and Realities of Special Education Michael F. Giangreco
With wit, humor, and profound one-liners, Giangreco will transform your thinking as you take a "lighter" look at the often comical and occasionally harsh truth in the ever-changing field of special education. This extraordinary, carefully crafted collection of 110 cartoons will inspire and entertain while providing a scrupulous look into the absurdities and realities of all areas of special education. If you would like to add humor and "food for thought" to staff development training – these cartoons are just what you need! These full size cartoons may be reproduced for transparencies! A great gift idea for yourself or someone "special". #P101 $19.95 8 ½" x 11" 125 pages Special education teachers, trainers, parents and administrators.

INCLUSION: 450 STRATEGIES FOR SUCCESS A Practical Guide for All Educators Working in
Inclusionary Settings Peggy A. Hammeken, M.Ed.
This perennial best-seller includes step-by-step guidelines to tailor inclusive educational programs to meet the needs of individual sites. Hundreds of ideas, tips, and strategies for all areas of the curriculum. Practical and easy-to-use!
Reproducible Forms! Teachers – all grades. #P100 $19.95 8 1/2" x 11" 144 pgs. s/c

INCLUSION: AN ESSENTIAL GUIDE FOR THE PARAPROFESSIONAL A Practical Reference
Tool for Paraprofessionals Working in Inclusionary Settings Peggy A Hammeken, M.Ed.
This comprehensive book provides everything the paraprofessional needs to work within the inclusive education setting. This resource is used nationwide to facilitate training and inservice for both new and experienced paraprofessionals.
Exceptional resource! Reproducible Forms! Teacher/Support Staff – all grades #P200 $19.95 8 ½" x 11" 145 pgs. s/c

INCLUSION: STRATEGIES FOR WORKING WITH YOUNG CHILDREN A Resource Guide for
Teachers, Childcare Providers, and Parents Lorraine O. Moore, Ed.D.
Hundreds of developmentally based, child-focused, strategies at your fingertips! Communication, large and small motor development, social/emotional development, pre-reading, writing, and math are only a few! Excellent resource for educators of early childhood and preschool and for those who teach older students will developmental delays
Reproducible Forms! Teachers/Parents - Preschool to gr. 2 #P301 $19.95 8 1/2" x 11" 185 pgs.

INCLUSION: A PRACTICAL GUIDE FOR PARENTS Tools to Enhance Your Child's Success in
Learning Lorraine O. Moore, Ed.D.
This resource answers many questions parents have about inclusive education and helps parents to promote their child's learning. Strategies, exercises, questionnaires, checklists, and do-it-yourself graphs are included. Emphasis is placed on collaboration between home and school. Reproducible Forms. Teachers/Parents – all grades. #P300 $19.95 156 pgs.

QUICK-GUIDES TO INCLUSION Ideas for Educating Students with Disabilities
Edited by Michael F. Giangreco, Ph.D.
This user-friendly guide offers essential information and brief, to–the-point advice for improving inclusive skills. The spiral-bound handbook consists of five Quick-Guides, each one devoted to a relevant topic such as: including students with disabilities in the classroom; building partnerships with parents; creating partnerships with paraprofessionals; getting the most out of support services; and creating positive behavioral supports. An excellent practical resource.
#B100 $21.95 160 pgs. 81/2" x 11" spiral bound

QUICK GUIDES TO INCLUSION 2 Ideas for Educating Students with Disabilities
Edited by Michael F. Giangreco, Ph.D.
This companion book to *Quick-Guides to Inclusion* presents pertinent information and advice on five additional inclusion topics: curriculum adaptations, instructional strategies, secondary transition, augmentative and alternative communication and administration of inclusive schools. This easy-to-use guide offers more ideas, tips, examples and suggestions that you can put to use immediately in your own school #B101 $21.95 160 pgs 8 ½" x 11" spiral bound

CHOOSING OUTCOMES AND ACCOMMODATIONS FOR CHILDREN (COACH)
A Guide to Educational Planning for Students with Disabilities
Michael F. Giangreco, Ph.D., Chigee J Cloninger, Ph.D., and Virginia Salce Iverson, M.Ed.
This manual provides a practical assessment and planning process for the inclusion of students with disabilities in general education classrooms. Features new, to this second edition, include a preparation checklist to familiarize participants wit the COACH system, a question-and-answer section to enhance communication between parents and professionals, and improved forms for planning and evaluating students' programs. With this user-friendly tool, educational teams will be able to identify the content of students' educational programs, incorporate programs into a general education setting, and pursue family-valued outcomes. #B104 $33.95 224 pgs. 8 ½" x 11" spiral bound 1998 2nd edition

INCLUSION: A FRESH LOOK Linda Tilton

Additional practical strategies and ideas to meet the needs of the diverse learners in classrooms today. Useful, concrete ideas. Many ideas which can be used "tomorrow". Appropriate for general and special education teachers at the elementary level. Great resource! #CC 100 $29.95 8 1/2" x 11" 224 pg. Teachers - grades 1-6

INCLUSION IN THE SECONDARY SCHOOL Bold Initiatives Challenging Change

Edited by Daniel D. Sage, Ed.D.
An exceptional compilation of case studies describing a variety of experiences with inclusive efforts at the secondary level Regardless of the success or the acknowledged difficulties presented by these 23 authors, there is much to be learned from the experiences of others. # NP 107 $29.95 272 pgs. secondary level

VIDEO   STANDARDS & INCLUSION: Can We Have Both?

Dorothy Kerzner Lipsky, Ph.D. & Alan Gartner, Ph.D.
The move toward higher standards in our nation's schools has raised a major dilemma for educators committed to the inclusion of students with disabilities. Drs. Lipsky and Gartner, from the National Center on Educational Restructuring and Inclusion at the City University of New York, address many of the critical issues facing educators who are supporting students with disabilities in inclusive settings. Visit schools across the country and observe first-hand how the learning needs of all students are being successfully met in general education environments. Learn how special education is a service not a location. Understand that the inclusion of students is not determined solely by where they are placed, but by their full and complete access to the same curriculum as the general education population. Whether a regular or special educator, this video is a must for pre-service and inservice training. 1998 #NP603 VHS, 40 minutes $99.00

COLLABORATIVE PRACTICES FOR EDUCATORS; Strategies in Effective Communication

Patty Lee, Ed.D.
Increase communication and collaboration skills with this great resource! With more than 60 strategies and 180 practice activities (individual, colleague, and group) this is the only resource needed to develop effective communication. Includes a set of *Ten Tip Cards to Help Reduce Stress and Increase Productivity in Daily Life.* All school staff – all levels #P302 $19.95 85 pgs. spiral bound

VIDEO   THE POWER OF TWO: Making a Difference Through Co-Teaching   Marilyn Friend

This video provides an in-depth look at co-teaching partnerships. Six different co-teaching arrangements are presented and discussed. Dr. Friend narrates the viewer though a five-step conceptual framework useful for novice co-teachers as well as experienced practitioners. Includes a 35 page Facilitator's Manual. #NP 608 1996, VHS, 42 minutes $149.00

TOUGH TO REACH, TOUGH TO TEACH Students with Behavior Problems Sylvia Rockwell

Prepare yourself for those encounters with the disruptive, defiant, hostile student by knowing how to defuse undesirable behaviors and structure "face saving" alternatives. This book offers lists of tips covering the following areas; setting limits, arranging the classroom for safety, providing a sense of purpose, dealing with parents, maximizing personal effectiveness and minimizing stress. This publication is filled with a variety of sample forms. A valuable resource for both general and special education teachers. #CEC 103 $24.00 106 pgs s/c

BACK OFF, COOL DOWN, TRY AGAIN Teaching Students How to control Aggressive Behaviors

Sylvia Rockwell
A vividly descriptive primer on how to work with groups of students with behavior or emotional problems, using the stages of group development as the basis for classroom management. This book includes reproducible behavior management forms, as well as instructional planning forms. Strategies for documentation and consultation are presented.
#CEC104 $27.00 144 pgs. s/c

TEACHING KIDS WITH LEARNING DIFFICULTIES IN THE REGULAR CLASSROOM
Strategies and Techniques Every Teacher Can Use to Challenge & Motivate Struggling Students
Susan Winebrenner
Step-by-step strategies, teacher tested techniques, and easy-to-use activities to benefit all students, without remediating, watering down content, or depriving your regular education students of the time and attention needed. Reproducible Forms! #FS 100 $27.95 8 1/2" x 11" 248 pgs. Teachers – all grades.

CROSSOVER CHILDREN A Sourcebook for Helping Children Who Are Gifted and Learning Disabled

Marlene Bireley
Educators and parents alike are challenged by children who are obviously intelligent but fail to make normal academic gains or are labeled "behavior problems." In this helpful encouraging book, a life long educator and expert on exceptional children describes the unique characteristics of "crossover learners" – children and youth who are both gifted and learning disabled. She explains how to select, adapt, and implement appropriate instructional strategies and materials, describes ways to deal with the immediate social/behavioral, intervention, and enrichment needs of gifted/LD learners, and offers instructional content and practice. Published by the Council for Exceptional Children.
#CEC100 #27.95 8 ½" x 11" 104 pgs.

ADD AND ADHD RESOURCES

LIVING WITH ADHD: A Practical Guide to Coping with Attention Deficit Hyperactivity Disorders
Rebecca Kajander, CPNP, MPH
This friendly, encouraging book is the perfect place to start for those who would like to learn more about ADHD. Practical, easy-to-use tips to help educators, parents and students cope with home, school, and social settings. A list of resources for parents and educators is included. #N100 $9.95 7 1/4" x 10" 72 pgs. Teachers/Parents - All Levels

TEENAGERS WITH ADD A Parents Guide
Chris A Zeigler Dendy, M.S.
Complete coverage of issues and challenges faced by teens with ADD, their families, teachers, and treatment professionals. Includes information related to treatments, intervention strategies, and advocacy. Although the title states parents – this comprehensive resource is a valuable tool for all educators. #WP 100 $18.95 8 1/2" x 11" 370 pgs. Teachers/Parents - Grades 7 – 12

THE MYTH OF THE ADD CHILD 50 Ways to Improve Your Child's Behavior and Attention Span Without Drugs, Labels, or Coercion Thomas Armstrong Ph.D.
Dr. Armstrong offers fifty non-drug strategies for helping a child overcome attention and behavioral problems. These include activities for increasing self-esteem and making the most of vitality and creativity. He also provides a checklist to find the interventions that are best for each particular child, and hundreds of resources – books and organizations – that support these fifty strategies. #NP104 H $23.95 HC #NP104 $13.95 S/C $13.95 303 pgs

HOW TO REACH & TEACH ADD/ADHD CHILDREN: Practical Techniques and Strategies for Grades K-8 Sandra Rief
Classroom-tested strategies, techniques and interventions at your fingertips to help children with ADD/ADHD. Superb comprehensive guide for elementary - middle school. #PH 100 $27.95 8 1/2" x 11" 240 pgs. Teachers - grades K – 8

If you have questions, would like to place an order or request a catalog feel free to contact us by mail, e-mail, telephone or fax. We will be happy to assist you.

Peytral Publications, Inc.
PO Box 1162
Minnetonka, MN 55345

To place an order call toll-free 1-877-PEYTRAL
All other questions or inquiries
Call (612) 949-8707 or Fax 612.906.9777

We encourage you to visit our web site for the most current listing of new titles and perennial best sellers!

www.peytral.com